MAHIṢĀSURA

IN

ART AND THOUGHT

MAHIṢĀSURA IN ART AND THOUGHT

DR. UPENDRA NATH DHAL
Reader, Head, Department of Sanskrit
Utkal University, Bhubaneswar.

EASTERN BOOK LINKERS
DELHI :: (INDIA)

Published by :
EASTERN BOOK LINKERS,
5825, New Chandrawal, Jawahar Nagar,
DELHI - 110007

Ist. Edition : 1991

ISBN: 81- 85133 - 47 - 6

Printed by :
Orient Offset,
Delhi-110032

Laser typeset by :
Compu-Media-The D.T.P. People
43, Bungalow Road, Delhi-110007. ☎ 2911869.

PREFACE

During this study many people have contributed to its accomplishment. It is my pleasant duty to express a word of appreciation to them.

While I was preparing an article on Mahiṣāsura, I met Professor S.P.Singh of Aligarh Muslim University who first of all suggested me to develop it into a monograph and from time to time he used to encourage me to see it through the press. Dr. Karuna Sagar Behera, Professor Ancient Indian History, Utkal University who helped me in collecting materials from various sources and offered encouragement with kindness and erudition. I am grateful to both of them. To Professor Pushpendra Kumar, Professor of Sanskrit, Delhi University I am obliged for his help and encouragement. My former pupil Sri Madhusudan Misra and my present scholar Sri Chaturbhuja Satapathy, Lecturer in Sanskrit, Talcher College, Talcher, who assisted me in collecting up-to-date materials for the development of my thought. So I express my thanks from the core of my heart to both of them for their keen interest and cooperation in my humble endeavour.

Due to kind permission of the Directorate, Archaeological Survey of India, I was able to produce some of the photographs of the Sculpture, which prompted my study of the Asura. I also extend my thanks to the artists who drew the outlines from different photographs for the purpose.

We are also thankful to Sh. Sham Lal Malhotra, Proprietor M/s Eastern Book Linkers, Delhi-7, and his two sons, Sh.Ravi Malhotra and Sh.Deepak Malhotra, who have completed the present Project - A difficult task, with the pleasing and zealous mind.

Finally I dedicate this humble work at the lotus feet of the Goddess Durgā without whose blessings, the work would not have been conceived at all.

Bhubaneswar, Upendra N. Dhal
October, 1990

LIST OF ILLUSTRATIONS

Fig.12a Mahiṣāsuramardinī Panel in Mahiṣāsuramardinī Cave, Mahabalipuram, District-Chinglepet, 7th century A.D.

Fig.12b Mahiṣāsuramardinī, Sisiresvara Temple, Bhubaneswar, Orissa, 8th century A.D.

Fig.13 Mahisamardinī, Vaital Deul, ·Bhubaneswar, Orissa, 8th century A.D.

Fig.14a Mahiṣāsuramardini, Parasuramesvara Temple, Bhubaneswar, 7th century A.D.

Fig.14b Mahiṣāsuramardinī, Paramaguru Temple, Bhubaneswar

Fig.15 Mahisamardinī, Hanumanesvara Temple, Jajpur, Orissa.

CONTENTS

INTRODUCTION

Mother Goddess as the presiding deity of Śāktas arrests the attention of all. Of the various epithets and forms of the Goddess, Durgā or Kātyāyani (also called Candī or Caṇḍikā) is very popular in the length and breadth of the country. Studies on various aspects of her character in our mythology, religion etc., grew in bulk. And her visual representation is well depicted in our Art, and Sculputure. It is interesting to note that the very origin of her such incarnation (as Durgā or Kātyāyanī) is mainly due to her counterpart Mahiṣāsura, the Buffalo-demon, for which she is well-known as Mahiṣāsuramardinī or Mahiṣamardinī, the crusher of the buffalo-demon. This buffalo-demon is usually assorted with her in our literature, Art, sculpture etc. But it is unfortunate that in our earlier works he could not get his rightful place as he deserved. Rather he is pictured as an enemy of Vedic gods creating various impediments for their smooth-living as such, looked upon as their sworn-enemy. Because of rather jealousy not of hatred Mahiṣāsura is represented in very uncouth form having unusual traits in his character, but the mystery behind such relation is never attempted to be explored.

Before stating the aim and object of our study on Mahiṣāsura, it is imperative to take stock of the past study on the concept of Asura in general at first. Among the earlier references, the article of W.Norman Brown entitled "Proselytizing the Asuras" which appeared in the *Journal of the American Oriental Society* [1] in April 1919 seems to be earliest. In it the learned author has tried to show the enemity of Asuras with the gods and for that purpose he ramifies refernces from the Vedic texts. Later in 1926, A.Banerji Sastri made an intriguing effort to establish the historicity of the Asuras in a number of articles, which appeared in the Bihar and Orissa Research Society Journal.[2] He considers the Asuras as immigrants from Assyria, who preceded the Indo-Aryans in India and were the builders of Indus valley civilization (Harappa Culture). D.R. Bhandarkar[3] also takes the Asuras to be the Assurs or Assyrians and refers to their later settlements in Magadha or South Bihar as traced in the Śatapatha Brāhmaṇa and others. Besides number of articles on the concept, the recent major work of Wash E.Hale,[4] *Asura-in Early Vedic Religion*, (Ph.D.dissertation, Harvard University, 1980) is worth-noticing. The source material in it ranges from the Ṛgveda to the Brāhmaṇas. In the introductory part he has surveyed the suggestions offered by various scholars-eastern and western, on the meaning of Asura and is inclined to accept such meanings something like lord, leader etc., as corroborated by Iranian mythology. While Iranian works recognize Asura as divine and Daeva as demoniac, earlier Indian tradition records both the terms viz., Asura and Deva to qualify the same Vedic deity. The Vedic gods like Indra, Varuṇa, Mitra, Agni etc., may be alluded to in this context. But the subsequent change of meaning of the term Asura as opposed to god does not seem to be attempted. Such study from the point of view of comparative philology or comparative mythology may help us to proceed further.

From the religious point of view the demon has certain role to play and is worshipped along with the Mother Goddess Durgā. As a result the representation of the demon in varying froms along with the Goddess is well-depicted in our Art and Sculpture. Of the large number of discussions on the Images, the long and exhaustive article[5] of M.Seshadri entitled "Mahiṣāsura-mardinī, Images, Inconography and Interpretation" is very significant. In the process of tracing the evolution of the mother goddess the learned scholar has collected more than seventy plates of Mahiṣāsura-mardinī to illustratae his view point and has shown the stylistic development of images of Mahiṣāsura by the way. Another paper of no less merit is contributed by G.Von.Mitterwaliner[6] namely, "The Kusana Type of the Goddess Mahiṣāsuramardinī as compared to the Gupta and Medieval Types". Besides chapters on the images of Mahiṣamrdinī included in other works,[7] we come across two monographs exclusively on Mahiṣamardinī. The first maiden attempt by Vijaya Kanta Mishra to explore the Iconographic and Architectural importance of Mahiṣāsuramardinī in the Indian subcontinent is presented through his work,[8] *Mahishāmardinī* in 1984. And the other one[9] namely *Mahisāsurmardinī in Indian Art* is by Shantilal Nagar, a keen Curator of various museums. These two works on the Mahiṣāsuramardinī in Indian plastic art through the ages are interesting from the stand point of the study of evolution of the cult image, where Mahiṣāsura is represented as subservient to the cult deity, but the systematic development of his icon from stylistic point of view does not seem to be properly studied.

In order to analyse the complex character of an Asura one needs the anthropological approach to the same. In this respect K.K.Leuva's work entitled,[10] *The Asur - A Study of Primitive Iron-Smelters* seems to be a welcome addition. He took up the study of the Asura as a scheduled tribe of Netarhat plateau of Chotnagpur, Bihar and surveyed their customs, rites, economic and social conditions etc., to find out certain remedy for their upliftment. In the early part of his discussion, he has tried to prove with certain allusions that the Asura is a primitive tribe with definite cultural traditions but their earlier affiliation with the Asura of ancient age is simply referred to.

As a work of merit in the line may be taken *The Ancient Indian Culture Contacts and Migrations* of K.P. Chattopadhyaya.[11] The learned author has discussed the way of life of Asuras and their contact with the immigrant, Vedic Aryans. Due to such close contact, the two cultures are fused together, as a result one can come across such nice cultural amalgam, neither purely Asuric nor purely Vedic. For such analysis he has collected data from Vedic and Epic literature, anthropology, sociology, archaeology and the like. In a way he has tried to find out the way of life of the Asuras in the past and their changes due to such cultural contact and clash, but the study does not appear to be systematic in form and full-fledged.

Another work[12] of interest of the present century is *The Indian Asuras Colonised Europe* by K.L.Jain Vasasisya. The learned scholar has collected copious references both from the western and eastern mythology to establish his thesis that the Asuras of India, as a dominant race occupied Europe, Africa, Sumeria, Bablyon etc., in the hoary past. His study seems to illustrate simply the superiority of the Asuras over other nations of the world without looking into the other aspects of their character. Thus the work seems more subjective than objective and is aimed at as if to show the excellence of the Asuras at the cost of others.

So far as the study on an individual Asura is concerned, mention may be made of the significant contribution[13] of G.C.Tripathi namely, *Der Ursprung und die Entwicklung der Vamana Legende in der Indischen Literatur* (1968) in German. The erudite scholar has collected data beginning from the Vedas extending up to the Epics and the Purāṇas, all about the myths pertaining to Bali-Vāmana and has highlighted the character of the Asura Bali as a great benevolent king and a devotee of Śiva. Through Śiva Bhakti he could achieve the world domination etc. In such character portrayal, the mythico-religious aspect of his life appears to be more pronounced than the further development of his character under cultural and social milieu.

On the other hand in the present work attempts have been made to investigate the character of Mahiṣāsura as an important member of Asura community from socio-cultural, religious and ethnological point of view in historical outline. And for that purpose we have to dwell at length on such materials - literary, socio-cultural mythico-religious, and the like to get a full picture of the demon. Thus the source materials and their context form the basis of the study.

The present work is divided into four chapters to show the origin and development of Mahiṣāsura through different stages and ages. The first chapter deals with the concept of Asura not as an epithet of various Vedic deities or other characters but as social beings belonging to a distinct tribe having different culture and tradition, their interaction with Vedic, post-Vedic and Epic-Puranic culture and religion. The clash between the Asuras (masses) and the Vedic gods or people (classes) is interpreted as the opposition of two different cultures. The Indo-Aryans represnt the Vedic culture, whereas the Asuras a differnt one. The cause of such hostility leading to ultimate subordination of the Asuras to the Vedic people and fusion of the two at last are included in it.

Our Epics and the Purāṇas contain various myths and legends to depict individual gods and Asuras and glorify the activities of the gods at the cost of the Asuras due to various social changes and Brahminical influences. Under such background various anecdotes relating to the birth and exploits of Mahiṣāsura and his interaction with the gods and the goddess, Mahiṣamardinī as recorded in the Epics and the Purāṇas are dealt within the second chapter.

In the third chapter the covetous position of Mahiṣāsura in Brahmanical rituals especially in the Navarātra festival of the goddess Durgā is fittingly discussed. The deification of the demon as a devotee of the goddess, as a form of Śiva, her consort and his regular ceremonial worship with the Mother Goddess illustrate the process of assimilation of two cultural cross currents. In this context different myths are also taken into account.

Hand in hand with the worship of Mahiṣāsura on ritual occasions, he is found well-represented in our art and sculpture. The stages of development of the icon of Mahiṣāsura include the theriomorphic form, the human form emerging from the neck of the buffalo and the combination of man's body and buffalo's head. These types of images along with their representation in sculptures of different ages are illustrated with number of plates to show their stylistic variations.

This study deals with the origin and growth of the Asuras, their customs, faiths, beliefs etc., and their difference from the Vedic Aryans in general. So far as Mahiṣāsura, a leader of the

Asuras is concerned, his role as an Asura through the ages is duly analysed in the work. Relevant discussions in the work may help to remove such misconceptions that the Asuras are ugly, unusual in form, different from human beings and hostile to the divine beings and are in possession of all abominable qualities, which are not at all appreciated in the civilized society. And the assimilation of two cultures viz., Vedic and Asuric leading to their peaceful coexistence and coherence is illustrated through the study.

FOOTNOTES

1. W.Norman Brown, "Proselytizing the Asuras", *JAOS*, XXXIX Part-2 (April 1919), pp.100-103.

2. A.Banerji Sastri, "The Asuras in Indo-Iranian Literature", *JBROS* XI.1 (March 1926), pp.110-139; "Asura Expansion in India"; *JBORS* XII.2 (June 1926), pp.243-285; "II Asura Expansion by Sea", *JBROS* XII.3 (Sept.1926), pp.334-360; "V Asura Institutions", *JBROS* XII.4 (Dec.1926), PP.503-539.

3. D.R.Bhandarkar, "Aryan Immigrants into Eastern India", *ABORI* XII.2 (1931), pp.103-116.

4. Wash E. Hale, *Asura-in Early Vedic Religion*, Delhi: Motilal Banarsidass, 1986.

5. M.Seshadri, "Mahiṣāsuramardinī, Images, Iconography and Interpretation", In Half-Yearly *Journal of the Mysore University* N.S., Section A - Arts, XXII.No.2 (Mysore 1963), pp.1-28.

6. G.Von.Mitterwaliner (Munich), "The Kuṣāṇa Type of the Goddess Mahiṣāsuramṛdinī: As compared to the Gupta and Medieval Type". *German scholars in India* Vol.II. Edited by the Cultural Department of the Embassy of the Federal Republic of German, New Delhi: Nachiketa Publications Limited, 1976, pp.196-213.

7. Odile Divakaran, "Durga the Great Goddess: Meanings and Forms in the Early Period" forming Ch.20 of the *Discourses*

on Siva proceedings of a Symposium on the Nature of Religious Imagery, Bombay: Vakil, Feffer & Simons Limited, 1984, pp.271-288; Bhagwant Sahai, "Mahisasuramardini" forming Ch.XIV of the *Iconography of Minor Hindu and Buddhist Deities*. New Delhi: Abhinav Publications, 1975, 181-195.

8. Vijaya Kanta Mishra, *Mahisamardini*, New Delhi: Rajesh Publications, 1984.

9. Shantilal Nager. *Mahishasuramardini in Indian Art*. New Delhi: Aditya Prakashan, 1988.

10. K.K.Leuva, *The Asur - A Study of Primitive Iron-Smelters*, New Delhi: Bharatiya Adimjati Sevak Sangh, 1963.

11. K.P. Chattopadhyaya, *The Ancient Indian Culture Contacts and Migrations*, Calcutta: Firma K.L.Mukhopadhyaya, 1970.

12. K.L.Jain Vasasisya, *The Indian Asuras Colonised Europe*, Delhi: Itihas Vidya Prakashan, 1990.

13. G.C.Tripathi. *Der Ursprung und die Entwicklung der Vaman-Legende in der indischen Literatur*. Wiesbaden: Otto Harrassowitz, 1968; another work on the same Asura has come to light since 1984. Due to non-availability of the text, nothing tangible could be said on it. The work is known as *"The Righteous Demon-A Study of Bali"* by Clifford Hospital, Vancouver: University of British Columbia Press, 1984.

CHAPTER I

GENESIS OF THE CONCEPT OF ASURA

The concept of Asura is no doubt a baffling one in Indian context, but it was equally well-known to some of the Indo-European communities of the world also.

Origin of Asura in Other Countries

The term is commonly conceived in our present belief as not-god or anti-god and is translated as demon. The 'demon' is derived from the Greek word 'daimon' (also called diamonion), which means generally a supernatural being or spirit in Greek mythology. This spirit was believed to be benevolent to human beings. It is said to have inspired Socrates, the great Greek philosopher to seek and speak the truth. In course of time it began to be applied to the lesser spirits of the supernatural realm, who exerted pressures on men to perform such actions that were not conducive to their well being. Then he was looked upon as malevolent one that forbodes evil, misfortune and mischief. Thus in Greek mythology and religion the demons were viewed both as benevolent and malevolent spirits as well,[1] but did not play any role under social context. On the other hand Asura or 'Ashur' is significant from Assyrian stand point.

By twentieth and ninteenth century B.C. Ashur (known in Akkadian as Ashur or Assur) was the national god of Assyria. The city of Assyrians is named after him. Further on, the term is used both as the name of the country and the people inhabiting therein. As he manifested as a political god, it was believed that he was responsible to bestow sceptre and crown. And the victory of the Assyrians was due to Ashur's blessings in multifarious ways.[2] The deity was represented through the symbol of winged disk. The Ashurs (people so called) associated to such a deity were noted for magic, medicine, sculpture, architecture and military prowess.[3] In subsequent age, Persians (Iranians) occupied Assyria. Though the Assyrians (Ashurs) were subdued, through their culture and civilization, they could win the Persians in other ways. The supreme deity of Assyria, Ashur Marduk appeared among Persians as Ahur Mazda or the Great Asura, thus cemented the alliance and continued the tradition which had already witnessed the exaltation of Marduk as the highest deity in the Babylonian pantheon. The people of Assyria continued to be identified as Ashurs or Asuras.

Ahur Mazda, the great god of light conveys the sense of 'good lord'. And his adoration was practised by the more cultured and steadier elements of the Iranian society. The language of the collection of their earlier work, known as Avesta of the Zoroastrians is closely allied with our old Sanskrit (the language of the Vedic Saṁhitās). This shows the earlier and closer contact of the Indo-Iranians and the Indo-Aryans. As a consequence one can mark deeper relation of these two cultures. But due to later developments certain changes are marked in these two. In India *deva* meant 'shining' (god) all through our earlier literary works, whereas in Iran the cognateword *daeva* throughout Avesta means demon (or perhaps false god in some Gothic passages) and Asura (Ahura), the deity in Iran is commonly used as 'demon'. But there is deviation in it, as a result Asura as an epithet was applied to important Vedic gods also. Iranians believe Asura as their god of light; except such theological consideration Asura does not seem to have any other relation with their society, whereas in India the problem appears to be different.

Since the structure of our study is dependent on the ongoing and continuous interplay of indigenous culture with that of invading Aryans, we have to depend on the earliest literary works of the Aryans like the Ṛgveda and the subsequent literary works, which extend up to the Epic-Puranic compositions. The period of composition of such works ranges at least from the second millenium B.C., if not earlier, up to the end of the Guptas. Since our emphasis is on the socio-cultural aspect of the Asuras visa-à-vis the Aryans, we have to take stock of the materials found also in archaeology, anthropology, sociology and the like. Then we have to move beyond the limit of the Vedic literature, and in the line the socio-cultural millieu as explored at Mohenjodaro and Harappa (well-known as Harappa culture) may be taken into consideration.

Origin of Asuras in India

To begin with, the Asuras are never mythical beings and their role was not simply limited to religious activities, but rather they belong to a historical people, whom the invading Aryans encountered within Indian soil.

Some scholars[4] consider the Asuras, the protagonists of Asura cult as immigrants from Assyria, who preceded the Vedic Aryans in India across the sea of salt water and were architects of Indus Valley Civilization. Others[5] try to identify Asuras with Sumerians (Babylonians) and establish their view point by tracing some of their customs among the Asuras, whereas another group of scholars[6] recognize them to have belonged to the undivided Indo-Iranian family, who lived in India prior to their immigration to Iran. The separation of the Iranians from Indians was attributed to certain schism between them. Since the hymns of the Ṛgveda were composed in the region of Saptasindhu, these two goups consisting of undivided Indo-Iranians are believed to have lived in that region (of Saptasindhu) before such great split took place. Whatever, may be their source of origin and their migration, it is certain that they were the earlier inhabitants of India whom the Vedic Aryans met with.

It will not be out of place to mention here the Asura inhabitants of present day to affirm their social existence. In the present state of our knowledge we meet with the Asura tribe inhabiting Netarhat Plateau, north-west corner of Chotanagpur, Bihar. They are reckoned now as one of the twentynine scheduled tribes of Bihar and are believed to have entered India through the ocean prior to the Vedic people and were pushed back by the larger and stronger goup of people due to various causes.[7]

Asura in Harappan Culture

As stated earlier, the Asuras or the Assyrians were behind the rise of the civilization and culture in the Indus Valley. It is said that Indra, one of the major gods of the Vedic people, who was called Purandara (destroyer of *pura* or city), was at the root of destruction of such prosperous civilization. This Indus civilization seems to have embraced vast areas like the whole of Sindh and Punjab, Madhya Pradesh, North Maharastra, Gujarat, part of Uttar Pradesh, Rajasthan, the valleys of north-west frontier province etc., or practically the whole of northern India and the west. The excavation at Mohenjodaro, Harappa, Kalibangan in Rajasthan, Lothal and Nageswara at Saurastra etc., has brought to light various aspects of life led by the inhabitants of those areas in the hoary past. Since the excavation was conducted basically at Mahenjodaro in Sindh and Harapp in Punjab at first instance, it was well-known as Harappa civilization or culture. The duration of such civilization, as revealed from its finds, seems to have lasted roughly between C. 2800 and 2000 B.C.

Harappa, though well-known as the centre of city civilization, was not completely unknown to the Vedic people. Indra's campaign against the Asuras is traced in the sixth Maṇḍaḷa of the Ṛgveda. There Indra is called the killer of the Asuras 'Asuraghna'. The RV.6.27 recount similar activities of Indra, the name of the Asura mentioned here is Varasikha, whom Indra overpowered together with his descendants. While Varasikha and his descendants are Asuras, their dwelling place is rightly the city of the Asuras, which is according Ṛgveda (6.27.5) called Hariyupiya.

Nowadays scholars are strongly inclined to identify this Hariyupiya of the Ṛgveda with the Harappa of the Indus Valley.[8]

Sāyaṇa in his commentary on Śatapatha Brāhmaṇa (1.4.1.34) has stated the city of Amarāvatī, the abode of the gods on the top of Mount Meru, beneath this Meru lies the city Irāvatī, where dwell Asuras. Between these two (cities) lies the earth. Though it is difficult to trace the tradition upon which Sāyaṇa depended upon, but the connection of Asuras with Irāvatī as suggested by Sāyaṇa cannot be simply neglected. On the other hand archaeologists have already affirmed such statement. The city Irāvatī (or the city on the bank of the river Irāvatī, modern Rāvi) has been identified with Harappa. Thus through such evidences it may not be difficult to believe that the Asuras were behind the growth of such city-civilization in the hoary past. Eventhough archaeological findings do not furnish us with direct evidences but some of the materials put forward by them may help us to trace the cultural millieu of the Asuras to a greater extent.

Asuras differed from the Vedic people in social customs. As for example take the case of the disposal of the dead between these two. From the excavations at Mahenjodaro three forms of burial are found out, among them the majority (about thirty) of which belong to complete burials. Such burial includes the inhumation of the whole body along with the grave furnitures, offerings etc.[9] Among the other types are found as fractional burials, and post-cremation burials, which seem to belong to tribes other than the Asuras, where Aryans might have formed part of the diverse population of those days. On the other hand the Vedic works would also focus further light on the custom.

Through such discovery the close relation of Indus people with Sumerians (Babylonians) and Egyptians seems very clear. Scholars are of opinion that either these inhabitants of Indus valley established close contact with those far off regions by the sea or they belong to a sea-faring people who came to India and developed such a rich culture. But it is certain that these Asuras were the early settlers of India prior to the advent of Vedic people. The presence of Paśupati or Yogīśvara and the cult of the Mother Goddess in Hinduism is attributed to these Asuras of the Indus Valley. Though not very clear, it is evident that the culture of the Asuras had difinite influence on the Vedic and later Vedic people and so on. Since the prehistoric materials seem inadequate, we have to depend upon the literary sources to study the origin and development of such culture.

Asuras in Vedic Culture

Apart from ancient material remains exposed by excavations, the Ṛgveda presents also some of the earliest Indian historical data, and other Vedic works also contribute equally for the purpose. Such vast literature includes the Ṛgveda, the Sāmaveda, the Yajurveda, the Atharvaveda along with their Brāhmaṇas, Āraṇyakas, Upaniṣads, Kalpasūtra and the like; the period of their composition extends from the C. 15th centruy to the 6th century B.C. or prior to the rise of Buddha. The three *Vedas* like the Ṛg, Yajus and Sāma belong to the classes whereas the Atharvaveda belongs to the masses, so the Atharvaveda imbibes the democratic or socialistic spirit than others.

The Vedic Aryans were a people of warlike stock breeders and were organized in tribes rather than in kingdoms. They followed a mixed pastoral and agricultural economy in which cattle played a very prominent role. The people settled in the regions between Yamunā and Satlaj, south of the modern Ambālā along with the upper course of the river Sarasvatī at the first instance. There they came in close contact with the indigenous inhabitants, who include Dāsas, Dasyaus, Paṇis and Asuras, the pre-Aryan tribes. But barring others the Asuras had significant culture of their own, which moulded our culture and society in the long run. In course of their peaceful coexistence the invaders often married indigenous women and had their offspring through such alliance. After a few generations the people became an admixture of Aryan and indigenous blood. Thus confusion of culture took place. But later the Vedic people battled with the Asuras for conquest, expansion and survival. Hence the tradition of the people gathered from the Vedic works not only speak of their earlier peaceful relation but also for their later supremacy, thus they evidence the cultural streams of both. The Vedic literature furnishes us with important information about the relationship of the Rgvedic Aryans with the Asuras to understand the structure of the then society and its cultural trends during such period.

The early phase is regarded as the period of dominance of Asuras over the immigrants. Such atmosphere is clearly reflected in the Vedic texts. Asura, then was used to mean human beings, friend and leader of the people: The Vedic seer implores Maruts to have a powerful hero who is an Asura of the people *(janānām),* a distributor, by whom they may cross the waters for a safe dwelling -

asme vīro marutaḥ susmy astu
janānām yo asuro vidhātā /(ṚV.7.56.24)

The Asura is portrayed here as a human leader of the people. An Asura having force of fighting men seems to be used as a friend to others:

anasvantā satpater māmahe me
gāvā cetistho asuro maghonaḥ /
traivṛṣṇo agne daśabhir sahasrair
vaiśvānaro tryaruṇas ciketa //(ṚV.5.27.1)

"The leader of the raid, the Asura, who is more excellent than any other persons, has given men two cows together with a wagon. Tryaruṇa, the son of Trivṛṣṇa, has distinguished himself with ten thousand, O Agni Vaiśvānara".

In view of their mutual understanding or superiority of the Asuras, the appellation 'Asura' was applied to the gods of the Vedic pantheon who were invested with highest dignity. Among those gods of Vedism Agni, Savitṛ, Mitrā-Varuṇa, Indra, Dyaus, Aryaman, Puṣan, Tvaṣṭṛ etc., are called Asuras:

Agni is implored as 'Father of sacrifices, Asura of the wise ones - *pitā yajñānāṁ asuro vipaścitām (ṚV.3.3.4)*. Agni as Rudra is also addressed as the Asura of great heaven, because he is identified with Rudra -

tvaṁ agne rudro asuro maho divaṣ tvam (ṚV.2.1.6)

Savitṛ, the sun as the great vivifier, generator and producer is twice called Asura -

tad devasya savitur vāryam mahad
vṛṇimahe asurasya pracetasah / (ṚV.4.53.1)

"We wish this desirable (thing) of the god Savitṛ, of the wise Asura".

Similarly the devotee prays Savitṛ, the Asura:

prati prayāṇam asurasya vidvān
sūktair devaṁ savitaraṁ devasya / (ṚV.5.49.2)

"Aware of the going forth of the Asura, favour the god Savitr with songs".

Asuraship is ascribed to Indra, the greatest warrior-god of the Aryans -

satrā madāsas tava viśvajanyāh
satrā rāyo'dha ye pārthivāsah /
satrā vājānāṁ abhavo vibhaktā
yad deveṣu dhārayathā asuryām // (ṚV.6.36.1)

"Fully yours are the intoxications known to all, fully the riches which are earthly. Fully you (Indra) became the distributor of booty when you assumed the Asuraship among the gods".

Among other gods of the Vedic pantheon, Varuna, in earlier mythology the supreme and sovereign deity but was superseded by the warrior-god, Indra, was believed to be the patron deity of the Asuras:

tvam viśvesāṁ varuṇāsi rājā
ye ca devā asura ye ca martāḥ /
śatam no rāsva śarado vicakṣe
'syāmāyumṣi sudhitāni pūrvā // (ṚV.2.27.10; 2.28.7)

"You, O Varuna, are king of all, both who are gods *(deva)* and who are mortals *(martā)*, O Asura, grant to us to see a hundred autumns. May we attain ancient, well-established life spans".

Mitrā-Varuṇa are called Asura -
imām̐ vām̐ mitrā-varunā suvṛktim
iṣam̐ na kṛṇve asurā naviyaḥ /

"I make anew this song like nourishment for you two, O Mitrā-Varuṇā, O Asuras".

Asuras are well-known for their *māyā* "occult power, magic, craft, deceitful skill, wile, special power, trick". The gods equally shared the same trait also. Mitra and Varuṇa are mainly connected with such power in the earlier stage. So Mitrā-Varuṇa are prayed for to protect the concept of Dharma, which stands for the fundamental order in social affairs and moral life *(ṛta)* with the magical power, which an Asura usually possesses:
dharmaṇā mitrā-varuṇā vipaścitā
vratā rakṣethe asurasya māyayā /
ṛtena viśvam̐ bhuvanam̐ vi rājathaḥ
suryam ā dhattho divi cittryam̐ ratham // (ṚV.5.63.7)

"O Mitrā-Varuṇa, who know the inspiration, you protect the vows with *dharma,* with the magic of an Asura *(Asurasya māyayā).* You rule the whole world with *ṛta.* You place in the sky the sun, the gleaming chariot".

Like the Asuras Mitrā-Varuṇa are in possession of *māyā*; so they are implored to cause rain through such power:
samrājā ugrā vṛṣabhā divas pati
pṛthivyā mitrā-varuṇā vicarṣaṇī /
citrebhir abhrair upa tiṣṭhath ravam̐
dyām̐ vṛṣayatho asurasya māyayā // (ṚV.5.63.3)

"Universal monarchs, powerful bulls, lords of heaven (and) of earth (are) excellent Mitrā-Varuṇa. With multi-coloured clouds you mount the roar. You cause the sky to rain by the magic *(māyā)* of an Asura".

Indra is also well-known for his māyā, who assumes manifold forms through it -

rūpam rūpam bobhaviti
māyāḥ kṛṇvānas tanvaṁ pari svām /
trir yad divaḥ pari muhūrtam agāt
svaiṛ mantrair anṛtupā ṛtavā // (RV.3.53.8)

"Maghavan wears every shape at pleasure, changing in his body effecting magic *(māyā)*. Holy one, drinker out of season coming thrice, through fit prayers from heaven".

Similarly Indra's *māyā* is illustrated thus:
rūpaṁ rūpaṁ pratirūpo babhūva
tadasya rūpaṁ praticakṣaṇāya /
indro māyābhiḥ purūrūpaṁ iyate
yuktā hyasya haraya śatā daśa // (RV.6.47.18)

"In every figure he has been the model: this is his only form for us to look on. Indra moves multiform by his illusions *(māyā)* ; for his Bay steeds are yoked, ten times a hundred." In subsequent stage of development such power was also attributed to other members of the Vedic pantheon.

The term *deva* the shining one, was used for the Vedic deities, who represent one culture and 'Asura' for another culture. But another interesting feature one can mark during the early age is the use of Deva and Asura in apposition for the same deity, which in later stage are opposed to each other. Rudra is called both Asura and Deva in the same mantra:
tamu ṣṭuhi yaḥ sviṣuḥ sudhanvā
yo viśvasya kṣayati bheṣajasya /
yakṣvā mahe saumanasāya rudraṁ
nāmobhir devam asuram duvasya // (RV.5.42.11)

"Praise him who has good arrows and a good bow, who rules over all medicine. Sacrifice for great well being to Rudra; favour the god *(deva)*, the Asura with prostrations".

It seems clear that the earlier Vedic Aryans led very peaceful life, respected the Asuras as their neighbours. In view of their superior or greater power the Devas renedered worship to the Asuras -

yathā devā Asureṣu śraddhām ugreṣu cakrire /
(RV.10.151.3)

"Just as the Devas rendered faithful worship to the powerful Asuras". Even a later Brāhmaṇa passage (*SB*.12.6.1.10 ff) furnishes us with a list of thirty three oblations to be offered with accompanying mantras to various deities in order to correct certain ommissions or commissions in a Soma ritual (expiatory oblations of Soma sacrifice). Among these deities Asura finds a place of honour. This clearly indicates the state of homogeneity between the Vedic people and the Asuras.

The epithet Asura applied to Varuṇa was extended to other deities. It seems such use was possible only when Asura power was dominant over the culture-bringers of Ṛgvedic folk referred to as Devas later. But such atmosphere might not have lasted for a very long time. The conflict for survival, expansion and conquest by the Aryans began slowly.

Basically the tribe of Asuras belongs to the earlier stock of the country. May be, they were of dark colour *dāsavarṇa* or the colour of the Dāsas. Since they belong to different culture, they could not accept the Vedic way of life, especially the gods of the Vedic pantheon and the performance of sacrifice. So they were known as godless or *adevayu*, non-believer of Indra *anindra,* non-sacrificer *ayajvān* and were not following the Vedic rituals *akarman*, or ordinances *avrata*. On the other hand the Asuras were the worshippers of dummy gods *mūradeva* and *śiśnadeva*. Like Paṇi, the Asuras spoke a strange dialect, and were called *mṛdhravāc.* This term is sometimes used for one who does not press Soma and does not speak the language of the Indra-worshippers (Vedic people) and is believed to be the natural enemy of the Vedic people. In this context the language of the Asuras may be taken as an illustration from the *SB* (3.2.1.23). According to it, during their fight the Asuras cry out *he' layo, he' layo (he' rayo, he' rayo)*, which means Oh ! the enemies.

Though the gods and the Asuras are stated to have sprung from the same parent, Prajāpati (*SB*.3.5.4.2), the gods are referred to be senior or elder and the Asuras, junior or younger. While the gods are said to have been created out of the upper breath of Prajāpati, the Asuras from his downward breath. Prajāpati, their parent, realised later that he had created evil from himself in Asuras, so he smote them with evil and darkness. Asuras had inherited *vāk* an admixture of truth and untruth like the gods but unlike them the Asuras preferred the untruth leaving the truth. After creation when the Asuras approached Prajāpati to advise them their way of life, he assigned them darkness and magic in view of their evil propensities which led to their ultimate ruin. So they are pictured as the malignant enemies of the gods, who always attempted to prevent them from performing sacrifice. As the Asuras had scant regard for sacrifice, they used to instal ordinary fire, which is used for the purpose of worming, cooking and burning.[10]

The conflict between these two groups is fully recognised in subsequent stages also. The earliest reference to it seems to be traced in the Aitareya Brahmana (1.14) of the C.8th or 7th century B.C. which tells us how the gods and the Asuras were at war and the gods were defeated. Originally the Asuras enjoyed a monarchical form of government having a king as their leader and head. As the gods were not so organized, they converged in a conclave and decided to have a king to lead them in battle. They appointed Soma as their king, then the tide turned in their favour soon. This Soma, may be the early priestly emendation of Indra (*AB*. 1.131.1; 1.174.1), who figures as the king of the gods in other contexts.

During the period of Asura dominance, the great gods of the Vedic pantheon were addressed as Asura. Indra, the warrior god of the Vedic people, who rose to prominence, was previously designated as Asura, but in the sixth Maṇḍala of the Ṛgveda we come across reference to Indra's campaign against the Asuras, as a consequence of which Indra was called there *Asuraghna*, the killer of the Asuras -

tan no vi voco yadi te purā cij
jaritāra ānasuḥ sumnam indra /
kas te bhāgaḥ kim vayo dudhra khidvaḥ
puruhūta purūvaso'suraghnaḥ // (RV.6.22.4)

"Tell us this: whether of old the singers obtained your grace, O Indra? What is your share? What is the strength - food of (you) the Asura-killer *(Asuraghna)*, O undaunted destroyer (?), much called on, with many riches". Thus Indra once an ally became a foe to Asura.[11]

A late hymn of the Ṛgveda (10.124) clearly speaks of the conflict between the Asuras and the Devas: During the conflict Indra took the lead. Then the gods like Agni, Varuṇa and Soma were the protagonists of the Asuras. But due to change of fortune, those gods joined Indra deserting Asuras. A legend from the Taittirīya Samhitā (2.5.1-2), which seems to have some points of agreement with the present one, may be referred to here: Tvaṣṭṛ created Vṛtra by means of a Soma sacrifice to revenge the death of his son Viśvarūpa (omniform), who was killed by Indra. When Indra was about to hurt his vajra at Vṛtra, Agni, and Soma, who were within Vṛtra asked him (Indra) to withhold his hand. Indra invited them to come out of Vṛtra deserting him and join his side. When the defection was successively accomplished Indra slew Vṛtra.

Of the three major deities, when Agni changed his allegiance and switched over to Indra's side, the Devas became *yājñīya* or with sacrifice, whereas the Asuras lacked it and were called *ajājñīya* or without scrifice. The father Asura referred to in the hymn (*RV*.10.124.3) is Varuna and used to have *māyā* or occult power, magic like the Asuras.[12] Thus Varuṇa is recognized to be the Asura Pitṛ, who was associated with the Asuras.

The role of Indra as the killer of the Asuras is very well remembered not only in the Ṛgveda proper but also in the Atharvaveda, Śatapatha Brāhmaṇa, the Gṛhya Sūtras and the Upaniṣads. It will not be out of place to cite an interesting instance from the Ṛgveda where Indra is also invoked to help his patron to obtain a share of booty from the Asuras, the enemy leaders :

yā indra bhūja abharaḥ svarvām̐ asurebhyaḥ /
stotāram in maghavann asya vardhaya ye ca tve
vṛktabarhisaḥ // (RV.8.97.1)

"O Indra, the pleasures which brilliant you took from the Asuras, (with these) enrich the praiser of this (deed), O generous one, and those who have offering straw prepared for you".

The battle of ten kings *daśarājñayuddha* also focusses further light on this : The war took place between Sudāsa, the Indo-Aryan ruler and the primitive settlers consisting of several autochthonous tribes like the Asuras and others for gaining power and superiority. The seer Vasiṣṭha supported Sudāsa, the ruler of the Bharatas, and Viśvāmitra the other ten tribes for their victory. The ten tribes include Anu, Druhyu, Puru, Turvasu, Yadu, Paktha, Bhalānas, Alina, Visāṇin and Siva and followed by others like Simyu and Vaikarṇa. The territory of Sudāsa lay between Paruṣṇi and Yamunā, somewhere about the regions watered by Sarasvatī and Dṛsadvatī.

Vedic scholars are of opinion that the battle of the ten kings mentioned in the Ṛgveda was between two groups, who differed in language and culture. The Purus, who led the ten kings were called *mṛdhravācan* speaker of incorrect or corrupt speech - *purūm̐ mṛdhravācam* - *RV*.7.18.13. Their opponents the Bharatas under Sudāsa were speakers of Aryan dialect (correct speech). This Puru belonged to the stock of the Asuras.[13]

As stated earlier, the Asuras had a different social set up and had matrilineal society. After the advent of the Aryans of patriarchal stock, intermarriage took place between these two groups. It will not be out of place to mention here Yayāti of Aryan stock, who married Śarmiṣṭhā, daughter of Asura Vṛṣaparvā. According to Vedic tradition, the children of such union should have been identified with the father's class. But because of their affiliation to their mother's kinsfolk, probably for accepting some traits of Asura culture, they are identified with them. Thus Puru, born of Yayati and Sarmiṣṭhā is stated to be an Asura. So far as the marriage custom of the Asuras is concerned, they differ from the Aryans characteristically. The M.B.D. type of cross-cousin marriage prevails among Asuras, which is not only found with them, but also continued among the Yadus. Baudhyana Dharma Sūtra (1.1.19,21), which seem to be pre-pāṇinian in age emphatically stated that the same custom was practised only by the southerners then.

Another very significant custom referred to earlier, is the rite of the disposal of the dead of the Asuras, which is very clearly illustrated through the doctrine of the self of the Asuras in the Upaniṣads. Such doctrine is cursorily mentioned in the Maitrāyanī Upaniṣad (7.10), but on the other hand Chāndogya Upanisad (8.7.1 - 8.8.8) clearly elaborates it in the episode of Indra-Virocana thus : When the gods and Asuras were given to understand by Prajāpati that the self or Atman which is free from evil, old age (or ageless), death, sorrow, hunger and thirst and whose resolve is real, whose conception is real, should be searched out and understood. Because the person having the knowledge of Atman obtains all worlds, fulfills all desires, both the gods and the Asuras desired to seek that Atman, by knowing which they will attain all the worlds and all their disires as well. Thereafter Indra from among the gods came out, so also did Virocana from among the Asuras to seek after it. Without communicating with each other both of them approached Prajāpati with fuel in hand.

Though there was enmity between the gods and the Asuras before, Indra and Virocana, who were the leader and king of the gods and Asuras respectively lived together peacefully for thirty two years, because of their eagerness to acquire this so excellent and precious knowledge. Seeing them leading the disciplined life of a celibate student of sacred knowledge, Prajāpati wanted to know the purpose of their stay there. Thereafter Prajāpati began to instruct them.

Prajāpti informed them that the person, who is seen in the eye is the Atman (self). Then they wanted to know whether, he who is perceived in water, or in a mirror, is the same Atman. Prajāpti clearly stated that he himself is perceived in all these.

The idea behind Prajāpati's statement is very clear. It is said that one who sees through the eyes and other senses, is the seer (*draṣṭā*) and Prajāpati meant him to be Atman, free from evil. But Indra and Virocana mistook this person to be the reflected image in the eye that is seen not the seer, and thus the true self is mistaken to be the body or the reflection-self. Though Prajāpati was right in describing the Atman thus as inside all, as the pupils were not yet of pure intellect, they misunderstood it.

As they were quite convinced that the reflection was the self, Prajāpati out of sympathy for their lack of understanding asked them to look at in a pan of water in normal dress and then with best attires. But they replied that they had seen their own reflection in different stages. Thus they were convinced of the indentification of the body with the self. When Brahmā could not remove their misconception, he was grieved at heart seeing them going away without the proper knowledge of the self and was sure, be they gods or Asuras, whosoever will follow such doctrine shall perish *-devā vā surā*[14] *vā te parābhaviṣyanti*. At last he bade both of them adieu with the hope that they would realise the true import of his words, whenever they ponder over it.

Later on being dissatisfied with such knowledge Indra approached Brahmā once again, but Virocana, the king of the Asuras rejoiced at heart and returned to his fellowmen. As he understood that the body, the shadow of which is reflectd in the eye, is the self or Atman, he preached the same doctrine, which is well-known as *dehavāda:*

Oneself (Atman) is to be made happy here on earth, oneself should be waited upon. He, who makes his own-self (Atman) happy here on earth, who waits upon himself - he obtains both this world and yonder -

ātmaiveha mahayy ātmā paricarya ātmānam eveha mahayann ātmānaṁ paricarann ubhau lokāvavāpnoti maṁ cāmuṁ ceti // (CH.Up.8.8.4)

As a consequence of such doctrine, the Asuras adorn the body of the deceased with enjoyable things, cloths and ornaments, for by this, they think they will win yonder world (or other world).

Therefore, even now here on earth they say one, who is not a giver *(adadānam)*, who is not a believer *(aśraddhadhānam)*, who does not perform sacrifice *(ayajamānam)*, is accepted by people as Asura *(asuraḥ vata iti): tasmād apyadyehāddanam aśraddhadhānam ayajamānam āhur asuro vate tyasurāṇām* (*Ch.Up.* 8.8.5). And such doctrine is believed to belong to Asuras.

The above episode also informs us that the Asuras do not perform sacrifices like the Vedic people and have no faith on gift or others like their counter parts. Moreover they follow the custom of inhumation or burying the dead under the earth with proper dress, ornaments and the like. Varuṇa, the great Asura, the ancestral deity of the Asuras in the *RV* (7.89.1) is prayed for not to send him so soon to the chamber of clay (cf.*AV*. 5.30.14). But the Ṛgvedic people were in the habit of burning the dead. Thus the difference between two races is clearly discernible from their beliefs and practices.

The Asuras knew the science of engineering, sculpture and architecture. Among them Maya is believed to be the greatest exponent of such Art. The Epics and the Purāṇas are replete with his achievements. A treatise on architecture and sculpture attributed to him is well-known as Mayamata.

They have control over waters (*RV* .2.143; 5.30.5; 1.103.2). They introduced irrigation, controlling and regulating the supply of water to their fields. They were depending on Agrarian economy but the early Vedic people depended on cattle-breeding. The Asuras were more materialistic in the sense of acknowledging the reality of the material human body and material universe around us and depending on their own resources, but the Vedic people were in the habit of depending on supernatural forces. The Upaniṣads clearly record such doctrine of the Asuras as *dehavāda* or identifying the self with the body (proto- materialism), and the idealistic understanding of the nature of the self of the Vedic Aryan simultaneously.

From the Vedic view of life it seems clear that two traditions were in vogue, which are widely different or diametrically opposed. The contempt for the Asuras by the Aryans at certain later phase is indeed well-known. The Asuras (sometimes identified with Lokayatas) were opposed to the Brahminical beliefs and practices. Such conflict must have been because of their rigidity on their own practices, which orthodox Brahmanism was in direct conflict. Thus the cause of despise of the Vedic people is clear.

Asura in Epic – Purāṇic Age

The Epic period of India, which ordinarily continues from the C.400 B.C. to 400 A.D., ushers in an era of cultural fusion. The faith of the centuries was crumbling down, the hold of the authority on the common mass was being shattered under such background, one can mark the society, where the Vedic and Asuric traditions are being intermingled together. The great Epics like the Rāmāyaṇa, the Mahābhārata and the Purāṇas bear ample testimony to such social conditions.

Besides glorifying Rāma, as an apostle of Aryan culture, the Rāmāyaṇa covers major part of it with the devastating struggle of the Asuras headed by Rāvaṇa, the representative of autochthonic culture. The character of Rākṣasa Asuras is painted as valorous, and wicked, revengeful, anti-social above all anti-Aryan in nature. Here the leader of such group, Rāvaṇa is related as the co-brother, of Kubera, son of the sage Pulastya (also called Viśravas). Hatred towards them is clearly represented through the traits of their character thus:

ucchettāram ca dharmāṇām paradārābhimarṣaṇam
sarva divyāstrayoktāram yajñavighnakaram sadā
Ram.3.30.12

The (Rākṣasa-Asura) transgressor of every moral law *(dharma)*, the ravisher of others' wives *(paradārābhimar ṣaṇam)*, the wielder of celestial weapons, the obstructor of sacrifice *(yajñavighnakaram)*.

The other Epic, Mahābhārata equally records the individual Asuras, leaders of the tribe and their assimilation into Aryan fold. They are elder brother of the gods born of Kasyapa and Diti and are called *Purvedevā* elder to Deva, and their opponent as well. The work also divides them into two categories like fierce and friendly *(raudrā maitrāś ca)*. It may be, those who accepted the Aryan culture, were taken as friendly and the other as hostile. Anyway their atrocities on others are very colourfully depicted there.

Intermarriage between these two tribes continues unchecked. Bhīma married Hidimbā, the son, born of their union, Ghaṭotkaca fought on behalf of the Pāṇḍavas in the Kurukṣetra battle. Aniruddha, the grandson of Vāsudeva married Uṣā, the daughter of Bāṇāsura. Pururavā's son Āyu married the daughter of Svarbhānu, an Asura. Not only the inter-tribal marriage was acceptabale, even the earlier Brahmanical law-givers went to the extent of including the custom of Asura form of marriage into their law-books and called Asura marriage. In such marriage, the bride was bought from her father by paying bride price.[15] The Vasiṣṭha Dharma Sūtra (1.35) recognises such marriage belonging to Manuṣa form. Though other sacred texts look on it with disfavour, the Arthaśāstra (3.2.10) allows it without criticism -

pitṛpramāṇāś catvāraḥ pūrve dharmyāḥ
mātṛpitṛpramāṇāḥ śeṣāḥ /

As for instance the marriage of Daśaratha of Rāmāyaṇa and Paṇḍu of Mahābhārata may be taken. Daśaratha of Ayodhyā married Kaikeyī and their son was illustrious Bharata. The sister of Śalya namely Mādrī was united with Paṇḍu on payment of heavy bride price (*Mbh*.1.105.4-5)

As stated earlier the emphasis on kinship through the mother was one of the dominant social features of the Asuras. For the purpose of their marriage, the male lineage is neglected; and the custom of MBD cross cousin marriage is welcomed. But due to fusion of Asura and Vedic culture, such new major social trend is accepted by the Vedic people. Among the Aryan tribes Yadus and others introduced it and Pāṇḍavas accepted it. Among the Yādavas the marriage of Kṛṣṇa with Rukmiṇī, of his son Pradyumna with the latter's cross cousin on mother's side may be referred to in this context. Of the Pāṇḍavas, Arjuna married Subhadrā, his mother's brother's daughter (daughter of Vasudeva).

Purāṇas also perpetuate the same custom, as a result we come across numerous such examples: Yayāti married Śarmiṣṭhā, the daughter of the Asura king Vṛṣaparvā and had three sons namely Druhyu, Anu and Puru. Because of his affiliation with the mother's side, Puru was called Asura. Siṁhikā, the wife of the Asura Vipracitti bore fourteen sons, who were called Saimhikeyas (*VāyuP*.68.17-19). The Asuras like the Paulomas and Kālakeyas are known after their mothers Pulomā and Kālāka respectively (*VāyuP*. 68.23-27). Kadru married Kaśyapa, a Brāhmaṇa sage (belonging to Aryan descent), her son Takṣaka and other snakes is mentioned as Kadraveya after their mother (*VāyuP*. 39.54). The sons born to another Asura wife of Kaśyapa, Khasā, are known as Khasāyas. The speech of Kaśyapa to his wife, Khasā, a demoness appears to confirm such suggestion, which states that a son is devoted to his maternal uncle.

All these very well affirm the matriarchal nature of Asura society.

The acute hostility between these two tribes is very well depicted in the Purāṇas. Sometimes the individual Asuras fight with the host of gods for supremacy, power etc., sometimes their atrocities are retailiated by the Asuras. Here also very interesting feature of the Asura's superior power is shown through penance: Madhu and Kaiṭabha practised austerities to annoy Brahmā, as they were intoxicated by the boon of the Goddess. Similarly Bāṇāsura, Hiraṇyakaśipu etc., were devoted to Śiva, Prahlāda and others to Viṣṇu, Tāraka, Durgama etc., to Brahmā for their favour. In such myths one can mark the mischievous role of other gods to spoil their hard toil or to destroy them by any means before they acheive their goal.

Asuras were a diplomatic and war-like people and had superior strength, so never bowed down under various circumstances. They always believed in the policy of exertion and hard labour, never hesitated to threaten the high gods or other such superior powers, sometimes to achieve their position, power and privilege. And ordinarily they could not be subdued by gods except in defeat or death.

The myths always try to picture them as evil, dark, causing devastating effect in the social order and they conclude by annihilating them by the gods to revive social order. The Devāsura legends in the later works may be mystically said to be the stories of the struggle between forces of light and forces of darkness the struggle which is believed to be a permanent feature in nature.

Among those, the celebrated Brahminical myth of the churning of the ocean is a popular one, where the Asuras seize the ambrosia, churned out of the ocean before the gods took possession of it. Similarly another myth of that category, popular among the adherents of the Śakti cult, is the Mahiṣāmardinī myth or the myth of Mahiṣāsura and his encounter with the Mother goddess. It points to how the Asura was powerful through divine favour and was ultimately subdued by the Mother Goddess, the combination of the powers of the gods. The myth in detail is to be taken up in the next section.

FOOTNOTES

1. *Encyclopaedia Britiannica,* Vol.I, pp.872 ff.

2. Tikva Frymerkensky. 'Ashur'. *Encyclopaedia of Religion* Vol.I, Ed. M.Eliade, pp.461 f.

3. A.Banerji Sastri. "The Asuras in Indo-Iranian Literature". *JBROS,* XII.1 (March 1926), pp.110 f.

4. A.Banerji Sastri. Ibid., pp.118 f; D.R.Bhandarkar also subscribes to the same view and identifies Asuras with Assurs or people of Assyria, who migrated to India, "Aryan Immigration into Eastern India"; *ABORI*, Vol.XII.2(1931), p.103f; D.P.Chattopadhyaya accepts 'Asura' as the personal designation of the tutelary deity of Assyria, which was used as a generic name by the Indo-Aryans, who must have come in contact direct or indirect with the Assyrians during the age of Kassites rule; D.P.Chattopadhyaya. *Lokayata,* p.56.

5. S.N.Dasgupta, *History of Indian Philosophy,* Vol.III, pp.528f.

6. P.L.Bhargava. "The Home of Aryans and Indo-Iranian Migrations". *ABROI.* Vol.48 & 49 (1968), pp.224 f.

7. K.K.Leuva. *The Asur*, pp.1 f.

8. M.Wheeler. *The Indus Civilization,* p.18; D.D.Kosambi, *Introduction to the Study of Indian History*, p.68; Cf.D.P.Chattopadhyaya, *op.cit.*, pp 57-58; Louis Renou. *Religions of Ancient India*, p.4.

9. R.C.Majumdar. *The Vedic Age*, pp.192 f.

10. G.V.Devasthali. *Religion and Mythology of the Brahmanas*, pp.50 ff.

11. Another account (*Maitrāyaṇī Saṁhitā* 4.2.9) to a certain extent corroborates such stage, which maintains: This earth was under an Asura and was rich with cattle. Indra conquered him and possessed the cattle; cf. *Ṛgveda* 6.27.4.

12. At present inhuman physical prowess and magical power are also believed to be in possession of Asuras, who utilise it at the hour of their need. Cf. Leuva. *The Asur*, pp.143 f.

13. The Puru of the Ṛgveda (7.8.4) and Yajurveda (12.34) is stated in the Śatapatha Brāhmaṇa (7.8.1.14) to be an Asura.

14. The opposition between the Asuras and the Devas by a sort of an etymology by which *a* in Asura is treated as a private particle and is interpreted in the sense of "non-sura". This even led to an erroneous formation of the word *Sura* to denote the gods in the Upanisadic age, if not earlier.

15. *Āśvalāyana Gṛhya Sūtra* 1.6; *Baudhāyana Dharma Sūtra* 1.35; *Gautama Dharma Sūtra* 4.12; Cf. *Manusmṛti* 3.31.

CHAPTER II

MAHIṢĀSURA THROUGH THE MYTHS

Our myths are encyclopaedic in nature. They convey our social condition, religious tradition, political behaviour, historical background etc., of the past. If the mythical or imaginative or speculative elements are extricated from them, the reality reveals.

The mythical literature, vast and varied, is traced in our Epics and Purāṇas. As they have been revised by various redactors through different ages, they represent our long span of society. As like other myths, the story of Mahiṣāsura does not escape such fate. We come across two sets of such myths of Mahiṣāsura in the Epics and the Purāṇas. One group of legend is intermingled with the story of Tārakāsura, whereas the other group appears along with the Mother Goddess Durgā (Kātyāyanī). The first one is related in the Mahābhārata and in some of the Purāṇas but the second one which is traced in large number of the texts appears to be very popular from ritualistic point of view. The earlier tradition, which is short and simple is accepted for examination at the first instance.

Mahiṣāsura and Skanda-Kārttikeya

The genesis of the first one is traced out in the Mahābhārata, the Vāmana Purāṇa and the Matsya Purāṇa. The story is recorded in the Mahābhārata twice, in one place in very short form, while in the other in a slightly elaborate manner. The Vāmana version develops the story further on, but the Matsya, seems to be of importance, records the Mahiṣāsura-Skanda myth as well as the Mahiṣāsura-Durgā myth. And it informs us how the second one grows slowly on the foundation of the previous one and appears to be a stepping stone to further development in bridging the gulf between the two.

The Mahābhārata records the encounter of Skanda with Tārakāsura twice, where Mahiṣāsura did not enjoy independent status. The shorter account (*Mbh.*9.45ff) states that Mahiṣa was an important warrior in Tāraka's army. Accompanied by his vast army of eight *Padmas,* Tāraka fought with Skanda and lost the battle. Mahiṣa, who was with them also met the same fate after ferocious fight. Thus ends the story without furnishing any details about Mahisa.

On the other hand the same work (*Mbh.*3.221.52ff) furnishes us with somewhat elaborate account of the above myth. It lays down that a terrible battle ensued between the gods and the Asuras headed by Tāraka. In the struggle Skanda-Kārttikeya was anointed as the commander-in-Chief of the celestial army. Gods began to crush the demons, as a result they were panic-stricken. At such hour of peril, Mahiṣāsura with a huge mass of rocks in hand rushed out of that terrible Dānava army, hurled it at the gods, as a consequence a section of warriors of the divine troop was beaten down the ground and perished. Indra and other gods fled away from the battle field. Mahiṣa was greatly enraged and advanced towards the chariot of Rudra and captured its pole by his hands. Overpowered thus, Rudra could not defeat Mahiṣa, because he (Mahiṣa) was made invincible due to Brahmā's boon. Thereafter Mahiṣa was delighted due to the possession of Rudra's chariot, but Mahāsena immediately advanced to Śiva's rescue, discharged a bright *śakti* to take the life of the demon. The weapon cut off the Asura's head, thus Mahiṣa met his doom in the battle. Gods were highly pleased and welcomed Skanda for his timely assistance.

The Mahābhārata accounts thus speak of Mahiṣāsura as a warrior of repute and is included in the vast army of Tāraka. In the battle between Tāraka and the gods, Mahiṣa like Tāraka was put to death by Skanda-Kārttikeya. Except this nothing is known about Mahiṣāsura.

The above legend of Mahiṣāsura appears to be revised and recorded in the Vāmana Purāṇa (31.1-32.1-11). Here Mahiṣāsura is represented as the brother of Tāraka and appears to have enjoyed superior or equal status to Tāraka. Like Tāraka he was a terrible source of affliction for the gods, so Skanda was approached to slay them:

mahiṣaṁ ghātayatv eṣa tārakam ca sudāruṇam //
(31.52);Cf.
skandasya vijayārthāya mahiṣasya badhāya ca //
(32.14b).

The story runs: Skanda was coronated as the commander-in-chief of the divine army to free the gods from the atrocities of Mahiṣa, Tāraka and others. When Skanda and his army landed on the ground there produced a tremendous roar. It alarmed the demons like Mahiṣa, Tāraka, Virocana, Jambha, Kujambha and others. They approached Andhaka for a secret conclave with him. In course of consultation, the demom Pātālaketu informed them how the enemies were drawing nearer to vanquish them and sought their protection. In the meantime Mahiṣa and Tāraka along with Bāṇa advanced towards the earth to face Skanda's challenge without the knowledge of Andhaka. A terrible battle ensued between the demons and the divine troops. Mahiṣa vanquished the Pramathas with the strokes of his club and pursued Kārttikeya. When Mahisa found Taraka slain in the fight by Karttikeya, he was afflicted at heart, terror-stricken he repaired to the Himalayas; Bāṇa also entered into the terrible repository of water.

Holding *śakti* in his hand on peacock's back Kārttikey followed Mahiṣa. Finding Guha chasing him, Mahiṣa left Kailāsa mountain on the Himalayas and entered Krauñca mountain. Because of his intimate relation with Krauñca, Skanda did not like to pierce him. But due to the interference of the gods, he was forced to do so. As a result the mountain was rent asunder and the demon Mahiṣa was killed -

jagmur divaṁ mahiṣam īkṣya hatam guhena //
(Vāmana 32.110)

Thus Mahiṣāsura, a warrior of Tāraka's army was done to death.

The same story of Mahiṣāsura undergoes further revision and elaboration in the Matsya Purāṇa. Alongside further growth of the myth it records acquaintance of the second one which seems to have been in the process of making. Here the version runs: Vajrāṅga and Varāṅgī were blessed with a son named Tāraka for favour of Brahmā. From his very birth Tāraka proved his valour. Among others Mahiṣāsura and Kujambha were so powerful as could lift the world. They anointed Tāraka as the sovereign among the Asuras -

abhiṣikto'suraiḥ sarvaiḥ kujambha mahiṣādibhiḥ /
sarv āsura-mahārājye pṛthīvitulanakṣamaiḥ //
(Matsya P.147.28)

Thereafter Tāraka continued severe austerities to be unvincible. Brahmā was pleased to grant him such a boon so that he would not be defeated by any gods but would fall a prey in the hands of a baby of seven-days-old. Thus invigorated with divine grace Tāraka directed the Asuras to prepare for the battle with the gods.

Grasana, the commander of Taraka army made preparation for the attack. Among ten commanders of the demon army are included Jambha, Kujambha, Megha, Kālanemi, Mathana, Jambhaka, Śumbha and Mahiṣa. The banners on the chariot of different commanders bore different symbols. Grasana's chariot carried the symbol of alligator *(Makara)*, Jambha's banner of the chariot was made of iron and imprinted with the face of a *Piśāca*. Similarly the banner of Mahiṣa bore the impression of a golden jackal - *mahiṣasya tu gomāyum ketor haimaṁ tadā bhavat /*

(*Matsya* 148.47a). Their chariots were also drawn by different animals. While Kujambha occupied a chariot drawn by hundread lions, Mahisa moved in a chariot carried by camels. Well-equipped with various weapons the commanders attacked the gods.

In such a bloody battle when demons were killed in number and Kujambha was rendered senseless, looking like the ferocious banks of clouds that gather to pour out volume of water at the time of dissolution of the world *(Kalpāntāmbhoda-saṁnibhaḥ)*, Mahiṣāsura shot the *Sāvitri* arrow, shining like flashes of lightning.

The missile dispelled the darkness of the sky resembling the autumn season. Thereafter the demons were enthused with renewed vigour. The battle continued. When Kujambha was about to severe Nirṛti's head with a sword, Varuṇa instantly appeared on the scene, tied down the demon's hands with his noose and began to beat him mercilessly. But the demon Kujambha took to the form of clouds charged with electricity due to vomiting blood. Mahiṣa rushed to Kujambha and tried to devour Varuṇa and Nirṛti. Understanding his intention they jumped down from their chariots and escaped to their respective quarters, but Mahiṣa doggedly followed Varuṇa. Soma darted his *Somāstra*, the store-house of chill *and Vāyavyāstra* towards the demons for the second time. As a result the demons began to shiver with cold and were rendered depressed and frustrated.

Afterwards when Kālanemi was defeated and asked by Viṣṇu to retire from the battle field, the demon army fell on Viṣṇu. He showered number of arrows on the demons, Mahiṣa began to cut them. So Viṣṇu took hold up his dreadful club and struck Nimi with it, but Grasana, Jambha and Mahiṣa smashed that. Grasana was killed by the quoit of Viṣṇu. When Mathana fell with the blow of Viṣṇu and other demons were dismayed, the terrible Mahiṣāsura indignantly came rushing forward to the field, attacked Viṣṇu with his trident and hit Garuḍa with his *śakti*. While trying to devour Viṣṇu with his carrier, he was knocked down to the ground with the help of his divine weapons. At last

Viṣṇu asked Mahiṣa to retire from the field for life, for he was destined to be slain at the hands of a woman as prophesied earlier :

> *mahiṣaṁ patitaṁ dṛṣṭvā bhumau provāca keśavaḥ /*
> *mahiṣāsura mattas tvam vadham nāstrair iharhasi //23*
> *yoṣidvadhyaḥ purkto'si sākṣāt kamalayoninā /*
> *uttiṣṭha jīvitaṁ rakṣa gacchāsmāt saṅgarād drutam //24*
> *(Mt.P.152.23-24)*

Instead of being killed Mahiṣāsura had to withdraw from the battle field.

The present version of the story appears to be an improvement over the Mahābhārata tradition. While taking note of the earlier one it tries to add new mlaterials to it to show the way for its further development. In earlier myth Mahisāsura is slain by Skanda-Kārttikeya but the Matsya further adds, the demon was only to be slain by a woman; even the great god Viṣṇu was not competent enough to kill him. Thus the version tries to make the path clear for the further development of the myth leading to Mahiṣa's annihilation by the Mother Goddess Durgā. And it serves as a bridging gulf between the earlier Mahiṣāsura-Skanda Kārttikeya account in the Mahābhārata and the Vāmana and the second one i.e., Mahiṣāsura-Durgā (Mahiṣāsurmardinī) in the Mārkaṇḍeya, the Varāha, the Śiva etc., of the subsequent stage.

In the present story Mahiṣāsura is pictured as a demon, probably Mahiṣāsura (A demon lord of the earth), in anthrorpomorphic form. But in the second myth, mostly he is stated in theriomorphic forms perhaps to find close resemblance between the name (Mahiṣa) and the form. The mythologiser's ingenuity probably was at work to provide such a form to justify his name only.

As to the sequence of the tradition it may be said that the story of Mahiṣa being slain by Skanda is recorded in the Mahābhārata and the Vāmana, but the popular myth hold Durgā responsible for his annihilation, the same form is also represented in our sculpture. In the earlier edition of the Mahābhārata[1] *(Virāṭa Parva, Ch.6 (Durgāstava); (Bhīṣmaparva, Ch.23 (Durgāstotra)* Durgā is extolled as Mahiṣāsuradarpaghnī. But the editors of the critical edition of the Mahābhārata have pushed them to the background on the point of its interpolation. Thus the Mahiṣāmardinī-Durgā tradition appears to have been of late origin. After analysing different Mahiṣāmardinī Durgā images in Art and Sculpture of different ages, D.C.Sircar,[2] is inclined to believe that since the earliest representation of it goes as far as the first century B.C., the episode may be of earlier origin than the image, but the tradition of Skanda-Kārttikeya as the destroyer of Mahiṣa is later than that, even though the Mahābhārat attributes the destruction of Mahiṣa more often to Skanda-Kārrtikeya than to Durga. If we accept the period of composition of the Mahābhārat, which ranges from earlier than the 4th century B.C. to the 4th century A.D. the Skanda episode may be put earlier than the Mahiṣāmardinī story. If Mahiṣāmardinī-Durgā tradition can be ascribed to earlier to 1st century B.C. at the latest, then Skanda story can be traced back to still earlier period. Thus the Mahiṣāmardinī-Durgā, though appears to be very popular in the age of the Purāṇas, seems to be posterior to Skanda story.

Mahiṣāsura and the Goddess Durgā (Mahiṣāsuramardinī)

The second tradition of Mahiṣāsura is traced in the episode of the Goddess Durgā (Kātyāyanī), well-known as Mahiṣāsuramardinī or Mahiṣāmardinī. The myth of Mahiṣāmardinī is popular than the Skanda myth and is related in the Purāṇas. The earlier myth does not deal with the birth and parentage of Mahiṣa, but the present one dilates on his birth and exploit etc., in an elaboate manner. Among the Purāṇas the Brahmāṇḍa Purāṇa (1.2.20.39) simply refers to Mahiṣāsura as an inhabitant of Rasātala and his destruction by the Mother Goddess Durgā. But the details of the myth is found in the Mārkaṇḍeya, the Varāha, the Vāmana, the Skanda, the Śiva, the Devībhāgavata etc. From the development point of view the story may be divided into two stages. The story of his birth and growth can be included in the first one, whereas in the second one his encounter with the Goddess leading to his annihilation would be taken up.

I. Origin of Mahiṣāsura

Of the above texts, the Varāha Purāṇa, the Vāmana Purāṇa, the Devībhāgavata, the Skanda Purāṇa and the Śiva Purāṇa record the birth story of Mahiṣa. The Śiva (5.46.1) simply refers to Mahiṣāsura as the son of the demon Rambha -

āsīd rambhāsuro nāma daityavaṁśa-śiromaṇiḥ/
tasmāj jāto mahāteja mahiṣo nāma dānavaḥ //

but does not go into details. On the other hand the rest of the Purāṇas contain four traditions of his birth.

Varāha Purāṇa Ch.95.1-22

The Varāha Purāṇa, which accepts a singular tradition narrates the story of origin of Mahiṣāsura thus:

During the primary creation, mightly sage named Supārśva, the friend of Sārasvata, was born out of water. His son Sindudvīpa was practising severe penance in the excellent city of Māhiṣmatī. Māhiṣmatī, the daughter of the demon Vipracitti in course of her pleasure trip entered into the hermitage of the sage with her friends. Finding the place very beautiful and charming she thought of possessing the same by driving out the sage, Sindhudvīpa. With this idea in mind Māhiṣamatī took the form of a she-buffalo and tried to frighten him. When the sage knew it, he became furious and cursed the demon's daughter to become a Mahiṣī (she-buffalo). As soon as they heard such highly injurious utterance, they began to realise the formidable nature of the offence and started repenting for their wantoness. After long supplication and entreaties the sage was moved with pity and promised her that her animal form would disappear only when she would give birth to a male buffalo.

Sindhudvīpa continued his penance on the bank of the Narmadā. Māhiṣmatī in the buffalo form also visited that area. Once it so happened that the sage, being overwhelmed with passion at the sight of a demon beauty bathing naked in the river, ejaculated his seed that fell in the river. And Māhiṣmatī drank the water carrying the semen of the sage. In course of time she gave birth to a son in the form of a buffalo. The son was named after his mother Māhiṣmatī and was called Mahiṣa -

tasyāḥ (māhismatyāḥ) putro'bhavad dhīmān mahāvala parākramaḥ// 21.b
mahiṣeti smṛto nāmnā brahmavaṁśavivardhanaḥ / 22.a
Varāh·P.95.21.22

Thereafter Māhiṣmati also got rid of the curse. The tradition of the birth of Mahiṣāsura appears to be singular and unaligned with any other myth.

From the above myth, it is clear that Mahiṣāsura was born out of the seed of the sage Sindhudvīpa through Māhiṣmatī in the form of a female buffalo, and had an animal form i.e., buffalo. It may be, such form was worked out to justify the name of the demon. It is equally interesting to note that the earliest representation of the demon in buffalo form clearly coincides with the myth.

Vāmana Purāṇa 18.42-60; Devībhāgavata 5.2.16-18

Another myth of the birth of the demon in buffalo form is related in the Vāman Purāṇa and the Devībhāgavata. The Vāmana dwells on the legend of Mahiṣa's origin at length in the context of eulogizing the *Viṣṇupañjarastotra*, while the Devībhāgavata narrates it to sing the glory of the Great Goddess (Mahāmāyā). In view of their similarity to a greater extent, they are taken up together thus:

Asura Danu had two sons, Rambha and Karambha by name. Both of them were issueless. They took to severe asceticism on the bank of the river Indus *(Pañcanada)* for long years to have a son. Karambha submerged under the water to begin with austere penance, but Rambha seleted the Peepal tree to worship fire under it. Indra in the form of a crocodile entered the water and devoured Karambha therein. When this sad news was communicated to Rambha, he was very much enraged. Wishing to take revenge, he determined to propitiate the fire god by offering his own head as an oblation in the fire. When he was about to cut his head for this purpose, the fire god appeared before him and prevented him from such heinous crime. He (Fire-god) was pleased with the devotion of Rambha and blessed him with a son, who would assume any form at will *(Kāmarūpī)* and would conquer the three worlds. And Rambha would be blessed with such a powerful son even through the female of any species.

Delighted at heart Rambha proceeded to a place of panoramic beauty in the company of Yakṣas. There his eyes caught a hamdsome she-buffalo, Śyāmā by name, who was maddened with passion. Without caring for any other beauty he desired her and she too gladly yielded to his passion. As a result of thier union the female buffalo conceived. The demon entered the nether world with her. Because of such unusual relation, his friends and relatives forshook him. So he left that region and lived with the Yakṣas.

As to the details of the birth of Mahiṣa the Vāmana differs from the Devībhāgavata. The Vāmana maintains : Being abandoned by his relatives Rambha lived with the Yakṣa Mālavata along with Śyāmā, his partner. There she gave birth to a fair-complexioned male buffalo, capable of taking any form - *ajījanat sutaṁ śubhraṁ mahiṣaṁ kāmarūpiṇam // 60.b (Vāmana P.18.60.b).*

Once another buffalo met her during her courses and wanted her union. Śyāmā being unwilling approached Rambha to save her from such situation. Then Rambha chased the bulffalo but was killed by him. That buffalo also entered into a lake to put an end to his life ; after death he was born as a demon, Namara and lived with the Yakṣas. Soon after Rambha's death, Śyāmā accompanied her husband, mounted the funeral pyre with him and perished. Out of that fire a great warrior named Raktavija was born. In course of time he (Raktavija) killed all the buffaloes, who came to his sight leaving the son of Rambha. That demon

Raktavija also conquered the gods later on.

This part of the myth is slightly changed and revised in the Devībhāgavata: When Rambha was killed by the other buffalo, who was attempting on Śyāmā, the Yakṣas, present there, also fought with him and shot him down. In the above version, Mahiṣa was born first, then his mother entered into the funeral fire of his father, but here, Mahiṣa is shown to be born from the womb of his mother after she entered into the funeral fire along with Raktavija:

mahiṣas tu citāmadhyāt samut tasthau mahāvalaḥ /
Rambho'pyanyad vapuh kṛtvā niḥsṛtaḥ putravatsalaḥ //47
raktavijo'pyasau jātau mahiṣo'pi mahāvalaḥ / 48.a
Devībhāgavata 5.2.47-48

Thus was born the buffalo-shaped demon, Mahiṣāsura who was said to be expert in changing his form at will. Like the Varāha tradition, the present myth also emphasises the birth of the demon in buffalo from, pure and simple, which corresponds to the earlier iconographical representation of the demon in sculptures.

Skanda Purāṇa (Brahma Khaṇḍa: Setumāhātmya) 3.1.6.1ff

As to the origin of Mahiṣāsura, different traditions are recorded in the Purāṇas. Besides above, we come across two different stories in the Skanda Purāṇa. One of them states:

when the sons of Diti were vanquished and humiliated by the gods, she was afflicted at heart, directed her daughter to perform rigorous penance to have a powerful son. As pointed out by her mother, she took to the form of a female-buffalo, continued severe austerity surrounded by five fires *(pañcāgni)*. As a result even the gods were terribly afraid of her. At last the sage Supārśva appeared before and granted her desire. As a consequence the son so born, would have the head of a buffalo and the trunk of a human being and would be named as Mahiṣa:

mukhena maḥiṣakaro vapuṣā nararūpavān // 14
mahiṣo nāma putrās te bhaviṣyaty ativīrjyavān / 15.a
Skanda p.3.1.6.14-15

Consequently the buffalo-faced-demon, Mahiṣāsura was born to the daughter of Diti and was crowned as king of the demons by Vipracitti and others.

Skanda Purāṇa (Nāgara Khaṇḍa) 6.119.1-39

The present work recognises another tradition of the myth, which differs from the above completely. The episode is narrated in the context of glorifying the Mother Goddess Kātayāyanī thus:

Hiraṇyākṣa (not Rambha as accepted in all other traditions) was blessed with a son named Citrasena. The child was very handsome and charming. From childhood days he was very much attracted towards the buffaloes. Leaving the horse and others he used to ride on the buffaloes. Once in course of hunting acquatic birds, Citrasena approached the bank of the river Jāhnavī. Unfortunately due to carelessness of Citrasena, the sage Durvāsā, who was performing meditation there, was injured. When the sage was unnecessarily disturbed in his meditation, he woke up and cursed Citrasena to turn into a buffalo as he hurted him with the help of such an animal and to remain dull so long in such form:

yasmāt pāpa mama kṣuṇṇam gātraṁ mahiṣajaiḥ khuraiḥ / /12
samādheś ca kṛto bhaṅgas tasmāt tvam mahiṣo bhava /
yāvaj jīvasi durbuddhe samyag jñānasamanvitah //13
Sk.P.119.12-13.

When he appologized for his misdeed the sage turned down his supplication and disappeared from the scene. As a consequence of the curse Citrasena instantly transformed into a buffalo and returned to his kingdom disheartened. Thereafter he approached Śukra for the remedy, who advised him to perform rigorous penance in Hāṭakeśvara Kṣetra to appease Śiva for the purpose.

As instructed by Śukra, the preceptor of the demons, he continued penance there. Due to his severe penance Śiva was pleased to grant him his desires: Citrasena in that form (buffalo) would enjoy all sorts of worldly pleasures in life. He would be so powerful that, except for one woman, nobody would be able to kill him :

striyam ekaṁ parityaktvā nānyebhyas tu vadho mama //34
Sk.P.6.119.34.b

Thus saying Śiva disappeared. Mahiṣa also returned to his kingdom.

It is clear that Citrasena, the son of Hiraṇyākṣa was born in human form, but due to his turn of fortune, he changed into a buffalo form.

From the above birth stories, it seems the idea of Mahiṣāsura as a demon was there. It appears to have been worked out in the mind of the Purāṇakāra to weave out the story of Rambha and Śyāmā leading to the birth of Mahiṣāsura buffalo-shaped, demon to justify the name. And such form in the Art and sculputre has very long antiquity. In subsequent stages other fanciful stories were fashioned with certain changes here and there to conform to such tradition. Thus the development of the myth proceeds through such stages from buffalo-form to buffalo-headed-human form leading to the change from human form to buffalo-form attributing a curse as the cause of such metamorphosis.

II. Mahiṣāsura's Contest with the Goddess

The battle between Mahiṣāsura and the Great Goddess is very interesting and illuminating. Because the Divine Mother Goddess crushed him in the fight, she was well-known as Mahiṣāsuramardinī. The encounter of the Goddess is recorded in the works like the Mārkaṇḍeya, the Skanda, the Varāha, the Vāmana, the Śiva, the Devībhāgavata etc. Due to revision and addition over the urkern, the legend appears in different forms in different hands, but the nucleus of the myth remains more or less the same. For the convenience of study it can be divided into two stages, the cause of the fight can be taken in the first part, whereas in the second part the battle proper may be dealt with.

-A-

The terrible fight between the Mother Goddess and Mahiṣāsura is well-known in the Purāṇas. But the cause of it differs one from the other.

Of the three causes, the first one seems to be very popular and is related in the Purāṇas like the Mārkaṇḍeya, the Śiva, and the Skanda. Accordingly the Asuras fought with the gods for power and position. The second one is described in the Skanda (6.11.9.75 ff), speaks of the battle by the Asuras for avenging the death of their kith and kin. Above all in the Varāha(92.1 ff) accounts the war is preceded by an episode in which Mahiṣa lusts for the Goddess and tries to seduce her. The classical account[3] runs thus:

Once Vaiṣṇavī Devī attended upon by female followers was practising penance. On his way Nārada met her, but was allured of her exquisite beauty. Thereafter he approached Mahiṣāsura, who was dwelling in a city close to the ocean. As Mahiṣāsura was already in possession of all the best choicest objects of the world, Nārada wanted him to master such a beauty, a jewel almong women. Being overpowered by passion he wanted to win her. So he called his ministers eight in number. One among them advised him to desist from such temptation, for she was no other than the Vaiṣṇavī Śaktī. Without caring for such counsel, he directed his commanders to declare war against the gods, climbing on an elephant Mahiṣa, himself also accompanied his army to the battle array. A terrible battle was fought between the gods and the Asuras, where the gods were miserably defeated and proceeded to Brahmaloka for succour.

Vidyutprabha, a messenger of Mahiṣāsura was deputed to woo her on his behalf. One of her followers Jayā by name suggested to depute one of them to satisfy Mahiṣāsura since Vaiṣṇavi Devi was observing *Kaumāra Vrata* then. But the messenger did not approve of it and went away. Thereafter Nārada approached the Goddess and related the miserable defeat and discomfiture of the gods by the demons and how Mahiṣāsura had become insolent due to the boon of Brhamā. At last he entreated her to annihilate the wicked demon at any cost and relieve the gods of his oppression. On hearing such sad plight of the gods, Vaiṣṇavī Śakti assumed terrible form and proceeded to fight with the demon.

The Vāmana Purāṇa (Chs. 19-21) tries to fuse the first cause and the third to make it a whole. Here the emphasis on the power and position of the demon superior to the gods is stated. Along with it his lust to get the Goddess as his beloved is given no less importance. The account[4] states:

Overpowered by Mahiṣa gods abandoned their abodes and repaired to Nārāyaṇa, met him along with Śaṅkara. They narrated before these great gods how their rights and privileges were usurped by the demon. Realising their humiliating plight, Viṣṇu flew into a rage like the fire at the time of destruction. Following Viṣṇu other gods like Brahmā, Śiva, Indra etc., issued from their face lustre of very high potency. The lights coming out of all these gods united in the Āśrama of the sage Kātyāyana and gave rise to the origin of the Great Goddess, called Kātyāyanī. Well-equipped with the divine missiles spared by the gods She dwelt all alone on the peak of the mountain Vindhya.

Once passing by her side, Caṇḍa and Muṇḍa,[5] the spies of Mahiṣāsura were charmed at the exquisite beauty of the Goddess. Immediately they communicated to their lord the bewitching form of the Goddess carrying formidable weapons of various kinds. Infatuated with love Mahiṣāsura made up his mind to get her by any means. The demon Dundubhi (Devībhāgvata calls him as Raktavija) was deputed as an emissary for the purpose. He related before Her the prowess of his lord and how he had brought under his control the three regions viz., the Heaven, the Earth and the Antariksa (intermediary region). He had usurped the powers of the gods of heaven; whatever jewels found on earth, in heaven or in the nether world were possessed by him. So She, being the jewel of womankind should accept him as Her Lord or master.

Thus addressed by the demon, Durgā-Kātyāyanī informed Dundubhi, the son of Maya that She was convinced of his valour and was prepared to accept him provided he fulfilled Her family tradition well-known as marriage present *(Śulka)*. According to it, he, who conquers the daughter of Her family in battle shall be Her husband:

yo jeṣyate'smatkulajāṁ raṇāgre
tasyāḥ sa bharttā'pi bhaviṣyatīti // 34 Vāmana P.20.34.b

Hearing the words of the Devī, Dundubhi reported all in verbatim before Mahiṣāsura. Thereafter the demon king directed his commanders equipped with the quadripartite army *(caturaṅgabala)* to chase Her violently.

The present version seems to combine both the earlier traditions, where his lust for possession of the Goddess becomes clear and such cause leads to his utter ruin.

-B-

The battle of Mahiṣāsura with the Goddess is narrated in different texts differently. But the short and simple version of the episode runs :

When Vaiṣṇavī Śakti was informed of the humiliations meted out to the Gods by Nārada, She immediately decided to come to their rescue. Assuming terrible form She accompanied Her followers to the battle field to face Mahiṣāsura. There the battle continued between Mahiṣa and Goddess. As a consequence Mahiṣa crushed all the Maids of the Goddess and proceeded towards the Divine Mother.

At the sight of the demon Devī became twenty-handed and held different weapons in Her hands. The battle caontinued for a pretty long time. Lastly Devī on the mountain Śataśṛṅga controlled the demon by Her feet and pierced him with the help of a spike *(Śūla)*. When She cut off his head with the sword, a male being came out of his body and proceeded to heaven:

tataḥ kālena mahatā śataśṛṅga mahāgirau /
padbhyām ākramya śūlena nihato daityasattamaḥ // 50
śiraś' ciccheda khadgena tatra c āntaḥ sthitaḥ pumān/

nirgatya vigataḥ svargaṁ devyāḥ śastranipātanāt // 51
Varāha P.Ch.94.50-51

The story does not refer to Mahiṣa's indomitable power through the favour of any of the high gods like Brahmā, Śiva etc., but states that the death was mainly due to his carnal desire for the Mother Goddess (*VarāhaP*. Ch.94).

On the other hand rest of the texts declare in unequivocal terms that the quarrel between the gods and demons was for supremacy and power. We beign with the traditions of Mahiṣāsura myth as it appears in the clasical record, the Devīmāhatmya of the Mārkaṇḍeya Purāṇa:[6]

When Mahiṣāsura was the lord of demons, the gods were defeated in a great battle by his host and were driven away from heaven. Accompanied by Brahmā, the gods approached the other high gods. From the energy *(śakti)* of the gods born of their fury, Devī became incarnate. Gods gave their divine weapons and sent Her for battle against Mahiṣāsura. Riding on the lion She uttered a loud roar blended with a horse laugh. By that penetrating roar, a great echo arose, all the worlds shook, the sea trembled, the earth quaked and the mountains moved.

Finding the three worlds greatly agitated Mahiṣāsura, uniting his army rose up together with lifted weapons and rushed towards that direction. He saw the Goddess pervading the three worlds with Her brilliance, causing the earth to bow low at Her feet and shaking the whole of *Pātāla* with the twang of Her bow-string. Then began the battle between the Goddess and the Asura hosts. The great heroes on Mahiṣa's side like Cikṣura, Cāmara, Udagra, Mahāhanu, Asiloma, Vāṣkala, Ugradarśana, Viḍāla etc., riding on horses, elephants or chariots etc., fought braverly. But the Goddess with her powerful carrier, lion faced the mighty forces with amazing destructive power. Ultimately the heroes fell one after the other in the battle field.

When the great army of the Asuras was brought to utter

destruction by Ambikā, Mahiṣāsura took up the challenge. His nimbleness, skill and strength were needed in the hour. In his buffalo form he terrified Her troops as a result some were laid low. After trampling the van of Her army he rushed towards Her lion. There Ambikā displayed Her wrath. Swollen with rage She looked on the great Asura and rushed on to slay him. She threw her noose over him and bound the Asura fast. As Mahiṣāsura was expert in changing his form at will, he quitted his buffalo shape when held bound and beame a lion suddenly. While Ambikā cut off his head, he took the shape of a man with scimitar in hand. Then the Goddess with Her arrows swiftly pierced the man along with his scimitar and shield. Thereafter Mahiṣāsura took the appearance of a huge elephant and tugged at her lion with his trunk and roared, but the goddess cut off his trunk with her sword. Finally he assumed his original buffalo form for the second time, shook the three worlds and hurled mountains against Caṇḍikā with his horns. Enraged thereat She exclaimed to slay him then and there. Leaping upwards She sat herself on that great Asura, pressed him down with Her foot on his neck and began to strike him with Her spear. That great Asura thus attacked, while partly emerging into human form, the Goddess chopped off his head with Her great sword and laid him low:

arddhaniṣkrānta evāsau yudhyamāno mahāsuraḥ /
tayā mahāsinā devyā śiraś chitvā nipātitaḥ //39
Mārkaṇḍeya P.83.39

While the Asura army perished with great lamentation, the gods were greatly exalted at this. Accompanied by the sages, the gods poured forth praises to the Goddess for removing their enemy on earth. Thus the great demon met his doom. The ultimate annihilation of the demon is recorded in most of the works.

These series of myths clearly impress upon us the idea of the encounter of the Asuras with the Gods and how the divine force ultimately come out victorious and the deomons sacrificed. Under social milieu, the demon represented a section of the society, who was not prepared to accept the Vedic way of life and was ultimately subdued and brought under control of the Vedic gods. As the above myths of the Purāṇas are Brahminised, the Asura epitomizes the dangerous, polluting forces at work in the world and his death at the hands of the Deity bestows his salvation.

Thus the Brahmanised Purāṇic texts have tried to rationalise Mahiṣa's death through allegorical interpretation. From all these, it is crystal clear that the myths represent the conflict of two sections of the society i.e, the Asuras and Gods for the superiority of the one over the other and for worldly possessions and pleasures.

FOOTNOTES

1. *Mahābhārata.* Gita Press, Gorakhpur Cf. Mahābhārata *(Virāṭa Parva)* critical edition, Appendix no.4, B.pp.300-304; *(Bhiṣmaparva)* Appendix I, p.710. Like Durgā Siva in the Mahābhārata *(Anuśāsana parva)* (Ch.14, 313) is designated as *Mahiṣaghna.* In view of its later interpolation the entire chapter is relagated to the Appendix I No.6, p.842 of the critical edition. Since Durgā was well-known by that time as Mahiṣamardinī, it may be Śiva might have accepted this appellation only when he was assorted with the Goddess as her partner.

2. D.C.Sircar, "Mahisamardinī Durgā, P.B.Desai Felicitation Volume, *Studies in Indian History and Culture,* p.155 f.

3. Similar cause is repeated in the *Devībhāgavata* 5.9.11; *Vāmana Purāṇa* 20.1-36; Cf. *Brhamavaivarta Purāṇa,* 2.16; *Devī Purāṇa* Ch.13.

4. Cf. *Devībhāgavata,* 5. Ch.7 ff.

5. These two emissaries of Mahisa are painted as the spies of demon Śumbha and Niśumbha in the *Devīmāhatmya* of *Mārkaṇḍeya Purāṇa.*

6. *Mārkandeya Purāna (Devīmahātmya)* Chs.82-83; *Devībhāgavata* 5.18; *Vāmana Purāṇa,* Ch.21.

CHAPTER III

MAHIṢĀSURA IN RELIGIOUS TRADITION

Mahiṣāsura in Religious Texts

Mahisāsura was the leader of an autochthonous tribe of the past. As the people of the tribe were hostile to the Vedic way of life, they were looked down upon and were branded as evil. That state of affairs continued for a long time. Ultimately when the Asuras were subdued, they gradually were forced to accept the Vedic way of life and fused with them. As a consequence of such amalgamation, one can mark the Vedic and the non-Vedic or anti-Vedic element in it, and in view of their overpowering popularity, the Asuras were never deprived of equal status with the Vedic gods. This state of affairs continues from the Epic-Purāṇic age, if not earlier.

It was customary with the Vedic gods to enjoy certain share in the sacrifice. In course of time due to various changes in the society, the place of sacrifice was occupied by the worship with various offerings and the *Bhakti Cult* cast a further spell on the way of life. As like other deities Mahiṣāmardinī Durgā accompanied by the Mahiṣāsura enjoyed due adoration. This position is very clearly recorded in the Śaktaite works like the Kālikā Purāṇa (Ch.61), the Mahābhāgavata Purāṇa (Chs.45-48), the Devī Purāṇa (Chs.21-23) and others. But the process of deification of Mahiṣāsura is very nicely related in the Skanda Purāṇa *(Nāgara Khaṇḍa)* and the Kālikā Purāṇa.

Interestingly enough the Skanda Purāṇa (Nāgara Khaṇḍa) (Ch.121) recounts the circumstances leading to Mahiṣa's elevation to the status of godhood thus:

After the defeat and discomfiture of the gods the Goddess was born of their energy and performed penance on the Vindhya mountain. Intimated by his followers the presence of such an exquisite beauty on the mountain, Mahiṣāsura, the son of Hiraṇyākṣa appealed the goddess Kātyāyani to accept him as Her consort, leaving such rigorous penance. But the Goddess in a fit of rage informed him how She was created by Brahmā to kill him and to relieve the gods of his atrocities. Incensed at this Mahiṣa challenged Her to a fight. In course of the dual, Kātyāyanī crouched on the back of the demon, but was carried away on the sky. The Goddess struck him at his back, as a result the demon began to bleed. And due to the severe attack of the lion at his back, the demon was rendered unfit to move. At this opportune moment Indra, the Lord of heaven entreated Kātyāyanī to behead the demon, failing which he would cause further disaster to the deities. While the Goddess was preparing to materialise their wish, the demon began to eulogise Her showering praises and prayers. He informed the Goddess how he was transformed into such animal form due to the curse of the sage, Durvāsā. Ultimately the Goddess took pity on him and was pleased to spare his life. Then the gods apprised Her the terrible consequence due to Mahiṣa, She assured them not to leave him but to put him under Her control for all time to come by grasping his tufts of hair with her hand -

nāham enaṁ haniṣyāmi tyajiṣyami tatha āmarāḥ /
enaṁ kacagrahaṁ kṛtvā dhārayiṣyāmi sarvadā //
Skanda Purāṇa 6.121.71

The gods were pleased at Her service and granted Her to be worshipped on earth on the back of the demon, Mahiṣa with a dagger drawn in Her hand in such terrible form:

sāmpratam martyaloke tvaṁ rūpam etat samāśritā /
śastrodyatakarā raudrā mahiṣopari saṁsthitā //73
atr āpsyasi parāṁ pūjāṁ durlabham amarair api /74.a
Skanda Purāṇa 6.121.73-74a

Thus the tradition continues unabated. And the demon, due to Devī's grace was saved and was granted a rare privilege of being honoured accompanied by Her.

In the next stage of development Mahiṣāsura is pictured as a devotee of Śiva, which is illustrated in a Śaivaite myth in the *Aruṇācala Māhātmya* of the Skanda Purāṇa:

Because of certain misdeeds Devī wanted to expiate Her fault. Śiva was pleased to direct Her to Aruṇācalam to continue penance in a hut in the forest. In order to get redress from Mahiṣāsura, the gods repaired to Her there and complained Her of his misdeeds. Goddess became angry at this and instructed Durgā to kill Mahiṣāsura in the battle. The battle commenced around the hut of the goddess at Aruṇācalam. With the wholehearted support of Aruṇānāyakī, four śaktis, eight Bhairavas and seven mothers, She defeated the demon army and cut off the head of Mahiṣa. To Her utter surpirse and horror, She discovered a bright *liṅga* upon the severed head of Mahiṣa.

Durgā carried the *liṅga* to the goddess, but when Devī took it, it stuck to her hand. Then the Devī could realise the evil of killing a devotee of Śiva and commanded Durgā to strike the mountain with Her sword. Water flowed out from it and Devī bathed in it for a month. At last the *liṅga* dropped from Her hand. Then the Goddess circumambulated that holy mountain. Thereupon Śiva appeared on the scene and granted Her request to occupy the left half of his body.

This version makes certain virtual changes in transforming the characters of Mahiṣa and the Devī. Since Mahiṣa was regarded as a devotee of Śiva, his killing became a sin of very heinous nature. Even the Devī is taught by the sage Gautama that it is wrong to harm any living being whatsoever (*jivahiṁsā na kartavya* - *Skanda P*.1.3.1.11.69). Because the victim is linked with Śiva as his votary, the crime of the Devī becomes far more serious; and the terrible nature of Her action stems from the transformation of Mahiṣa into a follower of Śiva, as shown by the *liṅga* on his neck.

The subsequent stage of development of the Mahiṣa myth is recorded in a later śaktaite work namely the Kālikā Purāṇa (60.85f), which serves as a guide especially for performing

Durgā's nine-day-festival in the eastern region of the country. The work highlights the adoration of Mahiṣāsura not as an adherent but as a form of Śiva thus:

It lays down, once while Mahiṣāsura was asleep at night on a mountain, he saw a very dreadful dream, where Mahāmāyā Bhadrakālī cleft his head and drank his blood. In the next morning he woke up. Scared with such ill omen, the demon began to worship the Goddess with his retinue for a long time. As a result of his propitiation, the Goddess appeared before him in the form of Bhadrakālī with sixteen arms, he bowed down before Her. In course of stating his dream before Her he also informed that he was cursed by the sage Kātyāyana to be killed by a woman as he had distracted one of his pupils with a beautiful image of a woman. He recalled, his father, Rambha formerly placated Śambhu, who promised that he would become his son in three births and rule the kingdom of the Asuras. Because of the curse he would be killed by the three forms of the Devī viz., Ugracaṇḍā, Bhadrakālī and Durgā.

The time limit of the curse is drawing fast. Mahiṣāsura is in possession of the three worlds, but needs more honour. As the Goddess was very much pleased with the demon, who was no other than his consort Śiva, She asked him to seek some favour. So Mahiṣa selected two boons, firstly, on account of Her favour he wished to enjoy a share in the sacrifice and to be worshipped in all the sacrifices; secondly, he longed to serve Her feet as long as the sun shines:

yajñabhāgam ahaṁ bhoktum icchāmi tvat-prasādataḥ /
yathā makheṣu sarvesu pūjyo'haṁ syām tathā kuru //104
tvat-pādasevāṁ na tyakṣye yāvat sūryah pravartate /
evam varadvayam dehi yadi deyo varo mama //105
Kālikā P.60.104-105

As the Goddess was appeased by the demon, She said, since the shares in sacrifices are intended for the gods, each one separtely, there is no share left to be given to him. So far as the second boon is concerned, when he would be killed by Her in the fight, he would never leave Her feet for ever. In places, wherever Her worship takes place, the worship of the demon in his corporeal form (buffalo form) would also be accepted.

kintu tvayi mayā yuddhe nihate mahiṣāsura /
na iva tyakṣyasi matpādaṁ satataṁ natra saṁśayaḥ //107
mama pravartate pūjā yatra yatra ca tatra tu (durmmate) /
pūjyaś cintyaś ca tatra iva kāyo'yam tava dānava
(varadānava) //108
Kālikā P.60.107-108; Cf.Durgāpūjātattva p.30

Lying at her feet the demon would be worshipped along with such forms of the goddess like Ugracaṇḍā, Bhadrakālī and Durgā, by the people on earth and in heaven by gods etc:

eteṣu mūrtiṣu sadā pādalagno nṛṇām bhavān /
pūjyo bhaviṣyati svarge devānām api rakṣasām //114
Kālikā P.60.114

And in view of his wishes the demon was allowed a share in the sacrifice later:

grahitvyaś ca paścāt tvam yajñabhāgopabhuktaye //117.b
Kālikā P.60.117.b.

and remains under Her feet for ever. Through three successive births Mahiṣāsura is identified with Śiva,[1] one of the high gods of Hinduism. The fusion of two culture like the Aryan and Āsuric seems to be completed by this time, which appears to be illustrated under such mythical garb. And Mahiṣāsura is admitted both into Śivaite and Śāktaite fold. Like the Devī, the demon is granted the favour by the gods to accompany Her in adoration. His relation with Śiva, either as a devotee or as a form of the deity, brought him a share in the sacrifice in later phase like Śiva. In this way the synthesis of the two traditions help both to form a new one, where the old is also allowed to continue.

Mahiṣāsura in South Indian Tradition

In South Indian folk religion, the character of a demon is very popular. He is pictured as devoted to gods. So the worship of demons and evil spirts is in various ways more prominent than the worship of the Brahminical or Purāṇic deities. Duc to spread of *Bhakti cult*, the demon is painted as a devotee, but symbolizes the evil within man viz., preoccupation with a false 'selfhood', the lust for power and opposition to divine ideals. The demon dies in the hands of a deity in order to be reborn through sacrifice and to achieve redemption thus.[2]

Among the demons in South Indian folk beliefs, not tinged with Purāṇic version, Mahiṣāsura enjoys a very significant position. D.D.Kosambi has drawn our attention to that buffalo-god called Mhasoba (Mhatoba) and his adoration in Mahārāṣṭra. In some areas, Mhasoba is married to Jogubai (Jogeśvarī or Durgā), whereas in other parts he is crushed by the Goddess. Either as a victim or as a consort, Mhasoba is adored in different parts of Mahārāṣṭra. Similar faith seems to dominate in other states of the South.[3] In Canarese country the buffalo is called *Gaudakona* or husband-buffalo. As tradition goes, the buffalo represents the outcaste husband, who pretended to be a Brāhmaṇa and married a girl of the Brāhmaṇa family. Now the girl is believed to be no other than the village goddess Uramma. And the buffalo dedicated to the Devī from the close of the last festival is sacrificed to the Goddess in the next festival, after which a fresh buffalo is always dedicated, so as not to allow the Goddess to remain a widow.[4] The Goddess is painted here as a murderous bride, who kills her partner after marriage. The legend also suggests the caste feud prevalent in the area by the time of the formation of such practice.

The position of the demon as a victim, without being united, needs further explanation. If we accept the demon as the manifestation of all evil qualities, how can he be worshipped? Due to the spread of *Bhakti cult,* the damned or the sinner is needed to be punished by the divinity, and through such punishment in the form of death he is believed to be redeemed from the present mould and get liberation from such state. Thus he turns to be a devotee, who gets equal adoration.[5]

The other way of elucidation may be sought from social point of view. The worship of the goddess began with the food-gatheres, whereas the god came to the forefront with the pastoral life. The union of the mother goddess with a male god is a phenomenon of the later conjoint society, where it became a necessity. But the opposition between a god and a Goddess is bound to occur in the early stage of development. On the other hand the South Indian tracts were peopled by such population, who had close affinity with the Asuras. So it appears to be usual for an Asura to rise to the position of a divinity to share certain privileges like the Hindu deities. Later on due to infiltration of new type of people with varied culture, clash between different cultures might have taken place. Under such changed atmosphere, though has to be victimised, still he retains his position and status of godhood as Śiva and is also revered as a devotee of the divinity or as an incarnation of Śiva.

Mahiṣa (Buffalo) as a Victim

Lord Śiva is identified with the buffalo-demon and the buffalo as well and is said to have become the carrier of the Goddess, as Her usual carrier, the lion was unable to do so-

harir harisvarūpeṇa na tvam voḍhum kṣamo'dhunā//151.b
mamāyam mahiṣah kāyas tava voḍhā bhaviṣyati/152.a
Kālikā P.60.151b-152a

In regular iconography buffalo is alloted to Yama, the god of death. The carrier and other elements (epithets and attributes) associated with a deity very well stresses the character of the divinity. Similarly the buffalo attached to Yama clearly illustrates his fierce character. The buffalo is generally accepted as a favourite object of sacrifice before village goddesses of South India in general and the goddess Durgā in particular.[6]

Here the question usually haunts one's mind as to why out of all animals, a male-buffalo is selected for sacrifice before the Goddess? The question seems to be well attended to in the folk myths of the South. In earliest Tamil sources, the buffalo symbolises power, valour etc.[7] The hero, who takes a bold stand in the battle against the enemies is said to have possessed Buffalo's valour.

The male god in the villages of South India is often called *Potu-Rāzu* or Buffalo-king, who is the husband of the village Goddess.[8] In certain sacrificial ritual a buffalo is married to the Goddess. After the sacrifice of the buffalo, another one is married to her immediately to avoid widowhood of the Goddess. There is an interesting folk myth which seems to justify the above action:

Once a Pariah (an outcaste) went to a Brāhmaṇa's village in the guise of a Brāhmaṇa and wished to study. There a Brāhmaṇa taught him *śāstras* for years. In course of time his (Brāhmaṇa's) daughter fell in love with him and married him ultimately. They led familylife and had children. In course of time Pariah's mother came to visit them. Before entering the house, her son got her shaved and dressed as a Brāhmaṇa widow and introduced her to his wife as deaf and dumb. On the other hand he cautioned his mother not to reveal his low origin. Once when the wife prepared a beautiful dish in which flour and water are formed into long strings, the old woman, instead of remaining silent, asked if it was the entrails of animals with which she was not unfamiliar. The daughter-in-law became suspicious and watched the behaviour of her husband and his mother. At last she was convinced of their low origin. Once she managed to send his mother-in-law and children away and burnt herself alive by setting fire to her house.

After her death the spirit of the dead woman appeared in the centre of the village as a divinity and accused the villagers of deceiving her. Warning for the dire consequences, she directed them to behead her husband, one of his hands should be placed into his mouth, the fat from his abdomen placed over his eyes and a light placed on his head before her. As directed by the deity the villagers took her husband around the village and beheaded him. Then the husband was born again as a buffalo and used to be sacrificed everytime. Such ritual continues every year.[9]

In a variant account of the same legend, besides, the other details it adds, one of the children sees his father stitching an old shoe before going out for a bath and informs his mother accordingly. When the mother comes to know how she was tricked, she transforms herself into Goddess Mari to be worshipped by low castes and curses her husband to be a buffalo fit to be sacrificed to her. Because of their low oɪigin, her children were cursed to be born as sheep and chicken. And during periodical Mari festivals, buffalo, sheep and chicken are used as victims; the right leg of the male buffalo is cut off and stuck in his mouth in commemoration of his having stitched the shoes in the guise of a Brāhmaṇa.[10]

The legend very nicely illustrates the role of the buffalo as the husband of the village Goddess and its subsequent victimization due to its treachery. Such sacrifice of the consort of the Goddess is believed at atoning one's misdeed. And such sacrificial killing of the victim-husband assures a fresh birth for the same purpose in the next time. Unlike the Purāṇic accounts, the present one attaches sin not to the wife, who burns herself to death, but her husband victim, who defiled her, whereby the murder is rationalised. This might have led them to call the buffalo as *Devarakonā* consecrated buffalo, husband buffalo *Devarapotu* 'devoted to the deity'.[11]

Besides such common practice the buffalo is specifically sacrificed to Durgāmmā or Durgā in South India.[12] Similar practice also continues in other parts of the country. The demon in the South Indian myths epitomizes the dangerous, polluting forces at work in the world. He achieves salvation due to his death at the hands of the Goddess. In some of the Brahminised works, his death requires an act of expiation on the part of the slayer, but the folk myth accepts him as a sinner. As such he symbolizes the evil within man with a false (selfhood) selfishness, egoism, the lust for power and opposition to the divine ideals. Due to the introduction of *Bhaktivāda* the redemption becomes possible only when the evil is destroyed. Thuṣ the death of the demon conveys two symobolic meanings, firstly, he offers himself in order to be reborn through the sacrifice; secondly, he dies in counteraction to the gods, thus gains his salvation. The demon becomes the object of emulation before humanity. The devotee immolates himself in a sacrifice either in imitation of mythical sacrificial victim, whose death transfers to the deity the power that activates the act of creation, which ultimately helps to restore the same victim, or in imitation of the demon, who is destroyed while still seeking more power. Thus the sacrifice of the demon through various stages of myths is rationlized.

Mahiṣāsura in Rituals

Because of different cultural affiliation, the Asuras remained in opposition to the Aryans and their divinities. In course of time with the decrease of Aryan immigration into India, the Aryan colonists and missionaries visited various unapproached areas and tried to win the good will of the natives by their superior knowledge and civilization. As a consequence the synthesis of the Aryan and primitive cultures began to operate, which provide scope for admitting other elements, hostile forces to come closer under the same banner. In course of time one can mark the multiplication of the Aryan pantheon due to the admission of the autochthonous elements.

Another factor that helped in such assimilation is the spread of *Bhakti cult* in the country. Once upon a time the Asuras were looked upon as the sworn-enemy of the Vedic people, but after the introduction of such faith, they were received as devotees, who needed salvation in life. That salvation was guaranteed through annihilation at the hands of Vedic deities. Thus due to various factors, the Asuras began to be admired by the Aryans; in the course of time they began to enter into their hierarchy to get due worship along with their gods. As a result, like other Asuras, Mahiṣāsura was admitted into the Brahminised pantheon. So later digests, ritual texts and other works began to incorporate him along with other gods.

Mahiṣāsura is well-represented in our religious digests and others, adoration to him along with the goddess and her *vāhana* is enjoined. In some works, the worship of Mahisasura follows Devi[13] in order, whereas in others it precedes the goddess, but proceeds the *vāhana,* the lion -

om mahāsiṁhāya namaḥ /
tato mahisāsurāya namaḥ iti mahisam devy agre pūjayet /
Varṣakriyā Kaumudī, p.436

The Kālīvilāsa Tantra (21.2) while laying down the *dhyāna* of Mahiṣāsura seems to attempt to justify his worship thus:
mahiṣas tvam mahāvīra śivarūpaḥ sadāśivaḥ
atas tvām pūjayiṣyāmi kṣamasva mahiṣāsura // [14]

Thus different works dealing with the paraphernalia of worship take due cognisance of the tradition and put due instructions for it.

From what has been said above, it is clear that Mahiṣāsura was put on a par with other Brahminical deities, when the fusion of cultures took place. But we have to mark one thing, that though the Aryan culture swayed over the Asuras and established its supremacy, the victor seems to be equally conquered culturally. As a result Mahiṣāsura is allowed due adoration, though in mutilated form, simultaneously with the Goddess. And the victim's position is also duly represented, which shows the fundamental significance of our culture, where old is allowed to continue along with the new one.

FOOTNOTES

1. The identification of Mahiṣāsura with Śiva appears to be very old. The three-faced with buffalo horns as his head dress in Indus seal is accepted by scholars as Proto-Śiva. This may lead to the conclusion that the pastoral buffalo-god, Mhasoba, is none else than Mahiṣāsura, whom the goddess Pārvatī crushed to gain her title Mahiṣāsuramardinī, D.D.Kosambi, *Myth and Reality*, pp.2-3.

2. Interesting and illuminating discussion is made on the plight of the demon in South Indian Temple myths in comparison to the classical Hindu myths in the *Tamil Temple Myths: Sacrifice and Divine Marriage in the South Indian Saiva Tradition,* pp.117ff.

3. D.D.Kosambi, *Myth and Reality*, pp.90f, pp.121f.

4. H. Whitehead, *The Village Gods of South India*, pp.72ff.

5. W.D.O'Flaherty has given a very convincing explanation to such motif from psycho-analytical point of view. For further discussion on the same refer to her interesting work, *Sexual Metaphors and Animal Symbols in India Mythology,* pp.81-86; 115-116ff.

6. Gustav Oppert, *The Original Inhabitants of India,* p.497, n.283; *Durgāpūjātattva* of Raghunandana (p.57) - states that the sacrifice of a buffalo to the Goddess, bestows longevity, wealth and fame - *āyurvittam yaśo dehi kāsarāya namo'stu te//* Cf. *Durgotsavaviveka* of Sulapani, pp.18-19ff. Following such tradition, in some temples in Orissa dedicated to Mahisāmardinī Durgā, a male buffalo is sacrificed during Navarātra festival which falls in autumn season every year.

7. The concept of buffalo symbolising strength is also traced in the Ṛgveda (9.96.6) *Brahmā...mahiṣo mṛgāṇām/* The well-known commentator Sāyana interprets Mahiṣa thus: *mṛgāṇām mahiṣo bhavati/ mahiṣākhyo balavān rājā bhavati.*

8. H.Whitehead, *op.cit.*, pp.18, 24,40.

9. W.T. Elmore, *Dravidian Gods in Modern Hinduism*, p.128ff.

10. H. Whitchead, *op.cit.*, p.84ff.

11. *Ibid.*, pp.78, 56, 62, 73.

12. Gustav Oppert, *op.cit.*, p.497ff.

13. *The Vaikṛtika Rahasya* appended to the Saptasasti states that after worshipping the Goddess, the devotee has to attend to the demon, whose body lies in the left side of the Goddess with severed head and then to the lion, the carrier of the Goddess in her rightside -

vāmabhāge grato devyāś chinnaśirṣam mahāsuram //29
pūjayen mahiṣam yena prāptam sāyujyam īśayā /
dakṣine paratah̤ siṁhaṁ samagraṁ dharmam isvaram //30

14. *The Bṛhat Ṭhākura Pūjāpaddhati* also records an invocatory verse addressed to Mahiṣāsura thus:

mahiṣāsura mahākāya devadarpa vināśaka /
tvat prakāśān mahāmāyā trailokyam samupāgatā //
p.206.

CHAPTER IV

EMERGENCE OF MAHIṢĀSURA IN INDIAN SCULPTURE

Mahiṣāsura is closely associated with Śakti Cult. The Navarātra festival of the Devī is usually observed in the bright half of the month of Āśvina and Caitra respectively. During this festival clay images of Durgā vanquishing Mahiṣāsura accompanied such other deities like Gaṇeśa, Kārttikeya, Lakṣmī, Sarasvatī etc., are worshipped with pomp and pageantry. At the conclusion of the ceremony the images are immersed in the river, pond or sea as the case may be. Besides this, images of Mahiṣāmardinī Durgā have survived as loose sculptures and latter ones have often remained in their original setting in temples dedicated to Śiva, Viṣṇu or the Goddess, where they are taken as part of an iconic programme. At times She is represented as *pārśvadevatā* in Śiva, and Viṣṇu sanctums but as main divinity in Sakta shrines etc.

Invariably Mahiṣāsura is accompanied by Durgā (Kātyāyanī) in her Mahiṣāmardini form in sculptures. But independent image of Mahiṣāsura is very rare. On the top of the Cāmuṇḍi hill in Mysore, Karnataka the lone standing image of Mahiṣāsura carrying a sword in the right hand and a snake in the left is found (Fig.1). The name of Mysore is believed to have been derived from Mahiṣāsura. As the presiding lord of the region he stands on the hill as if to protect the inhabitants from various dangers and calamities. In Maharastra Mhasoba (Mahiṣāsura) images are adored in different regions as like other deities.

The images of Mahiṣāmardini would show that various modes were followed in their representation. Multiple hands with emblems and attributes of the Goddess were accepted to be certain characteristic development of the images of the Goddess. Similar is the case with Mahiṣāsura. From the point of view of visual representation, the images of Mahiṣāsura may be divided broadly into two categories. To the first category belong the images of the Goddess, where the Devī subjugates the demon in animal form by breaking his spine and strangulating him with Her main hands, which carry no weapons. Here one can mark an implicit assertion of power of the Goddess without reference to a heroic deed, but the emphasis is portrayed with weapons, which do not appear to have played any part whatsoever in the battle. This type also tries to provide a clue to the old tradition, where She is called Mahiṣāsuramardinī or Mahiṣāmardinī, the crusher of Mahiṣāsura. The term 'mardinī' is derived from the root 'mṛd' meaning 'to press violently or to crush'. This act of squeezing the mighty buffalo to death in a close personal fight without bloodshed quite clearly responds to this class of Mahiṣāmardinī images. The representation of the animal form of the demon trampled by the Goddess ordinarily refers to very early group. A fragmentary miniature frieze of Mahiṣāsuramardinī, discovered in a village, Sanghel, South Gurgaon, Haryana may be accepted as an example. The sculpture depicts the demon in buffalo form. The Goddess is six-armed. Her front left and right arms are engaged in twisting the neck and back of the buffalo-demon with Her back right hand, She is holding the buffalo's tail, and Her two left hands are visible with mutilated objects. In view of its art style the use of red sandstone, the plastic execution, the poise and motion, the archaic features of the figure suggest it to the late Kuṣāṇa age.[1]

The rest of the images may be classed under the second category, where the explicit vision the triumphant warrior Goddess shows Her in action at the moment of Her battle with the archetypal Asura, Mahiṣa. In one of its variations, the demon is sculptured in buffalo-form, Devī carries such weapons like a shield, a thunderbolt etc., in Her two hands, but Her other hands, She catches the tongue of the buffalo in one and presses its back with Her other hand. The Goddess is active here to slay the animal-demon with the help of the weapons of war.

In another variety of the second group of images, the demon's statue is exalted, he assumes a human body instead of an animal. In this new bloody version, the animal is beheaded and the Asura is shown off half emerging from the severed neck of the decapitated body of the animal lying before. Here the demon in human form fight with the Goddess. In certain other the Goddess is shown in the act of slaying the buffalo-demon, who has the body of a man and the head of a buffalo, who is shown kneeling before the Goddess at Her feet.

In this category of Mahiṣāmardinī, the focus is on the terrible finality of Her power translating into punishment in the form of death itself, thereby inflicting the divine wrath on the personification of bestiality and evil that is Mahiṣa "Buiffalo". This tradition seems to continue from the Gupta period onwards in general.

Tracing out certain general characteristics of the images, scholars have tried to divide Mahiṣāmardinī into different types etc. But in case of Mahiṣāsura such generalization may not fit in. Though it is generally accepted that the earlier icons of Mahiṣāsura are depicted in buffalo-form, but deviations do occur very often. It depended on the choice of the sculptor to which tradition to adhere to. In later phases of development some earlier models are also adopted. In view of variations, deviations and additions or renovations in the images of Mahiṣāsura, they may be divided into three types to show their stylistic evolution through the ages. Accordingly the demon in animal form (buffalo) is included in the first group, whereas in the other he is shown as a human figure issuing out of the truncated body of the buffalo, but in the third group the demon is shown in human form with the head of a buffalo. In doing that we have not completely neglected the former suggestions of the earlier scholars, but we have to steer clear our way to show the evolution of the image of Mahiṣāsura through the sculptures. For that purpose we have to depend upon various sculptures found in the country for our study.

1. Mahiṣāsura in theriomorphic form

The composite form of the Goddess with Mahiṣāsura is scattered in the length and breadth of the country, out of which the buffalo-form of the demon is very interesting. The Devīmāhātmya of the Mārkaṇḍeya Purāṇa (83.20-26) speaks of his buffalo form in course of his combat with the Devī-

evam saṁkṣīyamāṇe tu svasainye mahiṣāsuraḥ /
māhiṣeṇa svarūpeṇa trāsayāmāsa tān gaṇān // 21
Mārkaṇḍeya Purāṇa 83.21

This type of images is found in various sites of the country.

Two votive tablets of the Mahiṣāmardinī listed in the catalogue of the Munich Museum under MU 199 and MU 200 (MU stands for Mathura) belong to the Kuṣāṇa period.[2] Comparatively older and better preserved one (MU 199) is of buff coloured sandstone. It depitcs the four-armed Goddess, Mahiṣāsura in the animal shape of a water-buffalo. The demon seems to have rushed towards the Goddess in front of Her, while the Goddess receives the fierce attack of the demon with his weight on Her right leg. Devī presses her right hand on his back and embraces him with Her left arm around his neck. Thus it creates the impression of wrestling fight due to the bodily contact with the animal. Of the other two hands, in Her upper or secondary right hand She holds a trident without shoulder pointing upwards likle the arm, while in Her opposite left hand sculptured inside view, She grasps a shield likewise represented in profile (Fig.2).

The second tablet (MU 200) made of reddish mottled sandstone found near Mathura does not appear to have been properly preserved. Though the Goddess is represented in almost the same attitude as in the previous one and the demon in the buffalo-form the way in which She overpowers the buffalo seems to have lost something of the vigour, displayed in the earlier one (MU 199). The forcible pressure of Her right hand to crush the spine of the buffalo is no longer present here. Due to certain variations in the posture of the shoulder, the sweeping curves of

Her legs, it seems as if She could hardly withstand the onrush of the buffalo in such a precarious position (Fig.3A, 3B).

If we take stalk of these votive sculptures of the Kuṣāṇa period, we find the Goddess overcoming the buffalo by breaking his spine and strangling him with Her main hands, which carry no weapons. And the weapons displayed in Her two upper hands are not portrayed in a position of immediate use in the combat between the Goddess and the Buffalo-demon. Instead of vanquishing the buffalo with any weapon, She subdues him with the mere strength of Her hands. The short-handled trident held in Her hand does not appear to have of any use to the Goddess to slay the demon.

The Museum at Mathura preserves a number of Kuṣāṇa plaques which depicts the Goddess combating Mahiṣāsura (buffalo-demon). Among the tablets of the period the beautiful Kaolin terracota plaque of Mahiṣamardinī found from the ancient site of Nagar (Malavanagar, Tonk district, Rajasthan) appears to be very old.[3] The plaque, now preserved in Amber Museum presents a sublime product of Indian artistic skill. Here the Goddess is shown with four hands. She carries a rectangular shield in the upper left hand a double-pronged thunderbolt in the opposite right. While within Her lower left hand She catches the tongue of the buffalo with the lower right She presses the buffalo's back. Here the earlier style of the Goddess has slightly modified, but the animal form of the demon continues unaltered (Fig.4A, 4B).

The reliefs of Mahiṣamardinī preserved at Udayagiri (M.P) belong to the early Gupta type; two are carved in front of Cave No.6, one on the north-wall of the courtyard and the other on the facade of the cave No.6 of the proper left of its entrance, whereas the third one is carved on the outside wall of the Cave No.17 at the same locality. In the first and third one the posture of the buffalo is represented as in the Kuṣāṇa type; the buffalo is still seen here leaping up in front of the Goddess, his head is rising above Her left shoulder, while She presses down his spine with Her main right hand. But in both She is seen mortally wounding the buffalo by piercing its back with the new long-handled trident *Triśūla* held by one of Her secondary right hands, whereas the shaft of the trident is badly defaced in the images of the Cave No.6, it is clearly traceable right up to its three prongs pointing downwards on the chime of the animal. On the other hand there is slight change in the relief on the facade of the Cave No.17. The Goddess, here, pulls up the buffalo's tail with Her second right hand, in the second left hand She holds the out-stretched left foreleg of the animal. The remaining hands, except the main right and left one carry weapons or atrributes.[4]

Large number of Mahiṣamardinī images are found at Bhubaneswar in Orissa. They mostly represent isolated sculptures, some of them are found in loose form and some are fixed to the walls of the temple. Reference to this type of image is found in the Mārkaṇḍeśvara temple.[5] Here the demon is in buffalo form and the Goddess is four-handed. She lifts the buffalo with one hand of the normal pair and thrusts the trident through the demon's body with the other (Fig.5). It is quite interesting to note that the description of this image to greater extent tallies with the Mahiṣamardinī-Virajā (at Jajpur, Cuttack district, Orissa) as related in the Virajakṣetra Māhātmya, which tries to glorify the Kṣetra along with the deities enshrined therein.[6]

The image of Mahiṣamardinī found in the Mārkaṇḍeśvara temple closely agrees with the icon in a niche of the Śiva temple at Bhumra (M.P.) ascribed to the sixth century A.D. The demon is represented here in buffalo-form. The Goddess having four-hands appears as standing with Her left foot disdainfully placed on the head of the buffalo. In one of Her left hands She holds the tail of the animal, in the other a shield, whereas of the two right hands, in one of it She holds a trident with which She pierces the body of the buffalo and in the other She holds a sword[7] (Fig.6). The image of the deity enshirned in the Vindhyavāsinī temple at Bhubaneswar may be taken as an example also. Here the Goddess is represented with four arms and the visual representation tallies with the above (Fig.7).

Thus we come across the image of the demon in theriomorphic form in sculptures of different ages. Either the buffalo is stiffled to death by the Goddess or he is pierced with trident or anyother weapon for the purpose. But the number of arms of the Goddess and the weapons held in Her hands vary.

2. Mahiṣāsura in half-animal and half-human form: complete Anthropomorphic form

The feature of the anthropomorphic shape of the demon coming forth out of the decapitated trunk of the buffalo is well-known as *Ardhaniṣkrānta* 'half-coming out'. This state is related in the *Devīmāhātmya* of the Mārkaṇḍeya Purāṇa (83.38 ff). The form of the demon seems to be very popular among the authors of Iconography and the Purāṇas dealing such section also. The iconographic texts include the Rūpamaṇḍana the Mānasāra and the Abhilaṣitārthacintāmaṇi etc. Of the Purāṇas mention may be made of the Agni (50.1-6) the Bhaviṣya .(*Madhyama parva*) 2.20.146.150) the Matsya (260.54-65), the Kālikā (59.12-21), the Devībhāgavata (9.50.68-70) etc.

Among the iconographical works on the type of the image, the Mānasāra[8] (C.3rd or 4th century A.D.) seems to be the earliest: The Goddess Kātyāyanī is said to have four hands, carries *cakra* and *Abhaya mudrā* in Her two right hands and Her two left hands She holds *śaṅkha* and *Varada mudrā*. She is conceived to be of dark colour (*syāmavarnāngā*) and is placed on a Bhadrapīṭha under which the decapitated body of the buffalo (*Mahiṣo hataśirah*) is to be placed. The other work of importance is the Rūpamaṇḍana,[9] which seems mainly to draw on the Matsya Purāṇa version.

All the Purāṇas recognize the Goddess (variously called Caṇḍī, Ambikā, Kātyāyanī, Durgā) invariably with ten arms. She holds such weapons like *śūla, vāṇa, śakti, khadga* and *cakra* in one side and in the other *cāpa, pāśa, kheṭaka, aṅkuśa, ghaṇṭā* or *kuṭhāra*. Due to the encounter with the demon by the help of such lethal weapons the head of the buffalo is entirely severed and the Asura should be sculptured as rushing out of that severed neck and carrying a sharp sword in his hand. Tied in the noose of snake the demon is pierced with a śūla-[10]

> *śiraś chedādardhajātam kabandhaṁ khaḍgaṁ/*
> *tīkṣṇam bibhratīṁ daityarājam /*
> *nāgaiḥ pāśairveṣṭayitvā samantā*
> *cchūlenaina nighnatīṁ dehamadhye //*
> *Bhaviṣya 2.20.149*

The demon, encircled by the noose of snake is held by the Goddess along with his hairs with Her hand. The breast being pierced by the javelin of the Devī, intestines coming out, the demon looks ferocious. While the right foot of the Goddess should be placed on the back of the lion and Her left toe should be shown touching the body of the Mahiṣa. Thus the *Ardhaniṣkrānta* form of the demon is represented in the form of instructions in such texts. The same instruction is elaborated in the Kālikā Purāṇa and bears testimony to its late composition.

The general adoption of a human form for the Asura is found scattered in various regions of the country with minor variations here and there. A stone sculpture of Mahiṣamardinī from Dulmi (Manbhum district) in the Indian Museum at Calcutta represents ten-armed Goddess fighting vigorously with the demon, who emerges out of the decapitated trunk of the buffalo. She stands in a *pratyāliḍha* pose. Planting Her right leg on the back of the lion, She presses the buffalo with Her left leg. She holds the weapons like the trident, *Kheṭaka, taṅka, śara* and *khaḍga* in Her right hands and *dhanu, paraśu, aṅkuśa, nāgapāśa* and *śucimudrā* in Her left respectively. Out of these weapons Devī pierces the shoulder of the demon with the trident held in the right hand and binds the demon's arms with the *nāgapāśa* in the left. The two-armed demon emerging out of the buffalo has still his leg within the trunk of the animal below, which is lying severed head and carried sword and a shield in his hand to fight with the Goddess[11] (Fig.8A,8B).

In the southern facade of the Jagamohana of the Liṅgarāja temple, Bhubaneswar, Orissa, an image of such type is to be found. In this representation, the victim is not a buffalo-headed demon, but a buffalo. From the decapitated trunk of the buffalo a male fignure is shown issuing forth[12] (Fig.9).

N.K.Bhattasali draws our attention to a ten-armed image of Mahiṣamardinī in the Dacca Museum. Though it is much akin in composition to the above, it differs in certain details. Besides the difference in weapons, the Goddess plunges dart into the demon's breast instead of a trident and subdues the demon by catching hold of his tuffs of hair.[13] The representation of the grasping of the demon by the Goddess is corroborated in the Agni Purāṇa and Kālikā Purāṇa account noted above.

The Ambā Devī temple at Jagat (South Rajasthan) appears to be a veritable microcosm of the Devī cult. Among different Ambikā (Durgā Mahiṣamardinī) images, reference can be made to two, one on the back side wall of the shrine and the other facing the east. Durgā is standing here in the *Āliḍha* pose with sword, arrow, *triśūla* and *aṅkuśa* held in Her four right hands and with *ghaṇṭā* (or *vajra* ?), bow, *pāśa* on the three left hands, while the fourth hand is holding the tuft of hair of a diminutive human form of the Mahiṣāsura shown coming out of the cut end of the neck of the buffalo form (Fig.10). The other one represents the demon entirely in human form, in standing position, challenging and combating with the Goddess. She is having the weapons in Her right hands respectively the drawn sword, arrow, *vajra* on three of her right hands and the *ghaṇṭā,* cobra, and bow on three left. With one of Her right hands, She grasps the left hand of the demon at the arm and his poised right hand (hoilding a mace) at the elbow. Her left leg is rooted to the ground and the right thigh and knee is raised up to naval level and flexed acutely with the foot pressing down the demon at his belly. On the other hand the demon in human form appears to have slightly lost his balance and caught firmly with his left leg obliquely planted on the ground flexed and raised to lion level. The lion mount, sitting on its hind legs holds the left leg to the demon at the knee with its claws and mauling him with its teeth. Thus the Asura in complete human form is represented here[14] (Fig.11).

3. Mahiṣāsura in human form with buffalo's head

We have already found the buffalo-demon represented wholly either in the form of an animal or in the form of a human being emerging out of the severed body of the buffalo or in complete anthropomorphic form, but the present type records certain remarkable changes in the form of human body with buffalo head by the demon, thus accepts the happy blending of the human and animal aspect reminiscent of the past.

A fine sculpture of Mahiṣāsuramardinī of this type is located in the first panel in the left courtyard of Kailāsa (Ellora Cave No.16). The demon has a human body but his animal form is suggested by his two horns on the human head. The demon holds a mace in the right hand and is ready for an attack on the Goddess. His left leg is lifted above. While he is on the right side, the Goddess is on the left. The eight-handed Goddess is seated on a tiger and holds a *triśūla,* a bow and an arrow in Her right hands, but the fourth one is broken. In Her left hands She holds a bow and a shield, the object in one is not distinct, whereas the fourth left hand is broken.[15]

One classic example of such image, rare in north India, is found at Mahabalipuram (also called Māmallapuram, Madras) on the walls of Mahiṣāsura cave (7th century A.D.). Here the sculptural representation of the Goddess engaged in a direct combat with the Buffalo demon is explicit. The relief appears to be a moving picture of a living battle, every line, every shade, creating the illusion of stirring conflict. It represents one of the masterpieces of the Pallava Art. Not simply representing the killing of the Asura in human form with buffalo head by the Goddess, it rather introduces two armies-one of Mahiṣāsura and the other of Durgā. Surrounded by the host of the Gaṇas, Durgā rides with firm grace on Her vehicle, lion rushing forward. The eight-handed Goddess brandishes different weapons in Her hands, using the bow with its string pulled up to the ear in Her attack against the demon. The crafty, powerful Asura seems to be on the defensive, is fighting with determination. He appears to have grown feeble, supporting and weighing the mace with both of his hands and waits for the opportune moment to strike the Goddess.

He is assisted by his army of Asuras, who are fleeing away, falling or seeking to escape. The umbrella held over the Goddess and the Asura king are the sign of royality. It also suggests that the demon has not yet been defeated but is moving away due to the shower of arrows from the Goddess and Her army. The scene leaves no doubt as to who would ultimately win (Fig.12A).

This type of images sems very popular in Orissa. The eight-handed Goddess is shown here as pressing down the head of the demon (buffalo-headed human figure) forcibly by the major left hand and thrusts a trident through his body with the main right. The other hands carry different weapons of war, like the sword, the shield, the bow and the arrow, the thunderbolt and the snake, and the snake is shown biting at the demon. The mount of the Goddess, takes active part in the fight and grasps a hand of the demon within the jaws. And the demon is depicted from the rear with his legs spread. Such images are found as *parśvadevatā* on the Śiśiresvara temple (Fig.12B), Vaitāl Deul (Fig.13), Paraśurameśvara temple (Fig.14A, 14B), and in two later temples on either side of the Bindusarovara, Bhubaneswar and in other places[16] (Fig.15).

To sum up: The images of Mahiṣāsura accompanied by the Goddess are placed into three modes. In one type the demon is represented completely in animal form, in the other is depicted in human form proceeding forth out of the neck of the buffalo or in human form, whereas the carcass of the buffalo lying there unattached. On the other hand the third type stands for the human body of the demon with buffalo head. But minor variations, here and there, are not uncommon.

FOOTNOTES

1. D.P.S. Punia, "Recently explored icon of Mahiṣāsuramardinī from South Haryana", *Vishveshvarānanda Indological Journal*, Vol.XIX, Pts.i-ii (1981), p.239.

2. G.V.Mitterwaliner (Munich), "The Kuṣāṇa Type of the Goddess Mahiṣāsuramardinī as compared to the Gupta and Medieval types", *German Scholars in India,* Vol.II,pp.196-213.

3. R.C.Agrawala, "Mahishamardinī in early Rajasthani Art", *The Researcher,* Vols.V-VI, pp.11-15.

4. G.V.Mitterwaliner, *op.cit.*, p.199 f.

5. K.C. Panigrahi, *Archaeological Remains at Bhubaneswar*, pp.133 f.

6. U.N. Dhal, *The Glory that was Viraja Kṣetra,* Ch.2.12-13.
viśvaṁcaturmukti ! sṛjasyatha rakṣasi tvam,
saṅkham rathāṅgam aniśaṁ dadhati karābhyām /12a
xx xx xx
vāhāriśirṣamaravindanibhena pādenākramya,
pāṇikamalena gṛhītpucchā/
anyena tat kakudaga triśikhasya mūlaṁ,
saṁgṛhya bhūṣayasi me haha gārhapatyam // 13

7. R.D. Banerjee, *Memoirs of the Archaeological Survey of India,* No.16, p.13 (Plate No.XIVB).

8. *Mānasāra on Architecture and Sculpture*, Ed. P.K. Acharya, Ch. 54.87-90.

9. *Rupamaṇḍana* of Srī Sūtradhara Maṇḍana, Ed. B.Srivastava Ch.5.45-50.

10. The same idea is represented in other works thus: *The Agni Purāṇa* (50.4)-

śastrodyatakaraḥ kruddhas tadgrīvāsambhava pumān /
śūlahasto vamad rakto raktasraṁ mūrddhajekṣaṇam //
Cf. śirascchedodbhavam tadvad dānavaṁ khadgapāṇinam /
hṛdi śūlena nirbhinnaṁ niryadantravibhūṣitam //
(Matsya P.260.62)

11. B.Sahai, *Iconography of Minor Hindu and Buddhist Deities,* p.186.

12. K.C. Panigrahi, *op.cit.,* pp.133 f.

13. N.K.Bhattasali, *Iconography of Buddhist and Brahmanical Sculptures in the Dacca Museum,* pp.197-198 (Pt.LVI).

14. K.V.Soundara Rajan, "A Devi Cult nucleus at Jagat, Rajasthan", *Vishveshvaranand Indological Journal,* Vol.I(i), p.134, 136.

15. R.C. Gupte and B.D. Mahajan, *Ajanta, Ellora and Aurangabad Caves*, p.126.

16. K.C. Panigrahi, *op.cit.*,pp.133 f; T.E.Donaldson, *Hindu Temple Art of Orissa,* Vol.III, pp.1063-1067.

CONCLUSION

In the preceding pages we have studied only the character of Mahiṣāsura, a leader of the Asura tribe and representative of one glorious civilization and culture of the past.

It cannot be gain said that the Asuras belong to a primitive race having definite way of life with characteristic faith and belief, for which differed from the invading Aryans, who entered India later. In course of time schism grew between them which led to their acute hostility. Despite the process of amalgamation of two cultures - Sura (Aryan) and Asura, their rivalry which seems echoed in the early stage, became more articulate at least by the time of Buddha. And the Vedic literature bears copious references to such social change.

The Epics and the Psuranas present the attitude of a segment of Brāhmaṇas, who attempted to reinterpret it to fit their partisan conception. As a result these works highlight the psychology of Brahminical writers. In the bulk of such texts Asuras no doubt are pictured stronger than their adversaries, the Vedic people and their divinities. Such antagonism led them to put an Asura as hostile to the gods, for which constant feud continued. Out of contempt and jealousy to their culture and society, they are portrayed as uncouth in form with undesirable social behaviour. This attitude led them to put Mahisāsura sometimes as an animal, sometimes as human being and sometimes the combination of both in one, but in reality he was a powerful warrior and out and out human in form. Because of socio-cultural difference and the atrocities of the Vedic people or gods for supremacy, he used to retaliate sometimes by degrading them from their status and

position. As he was superior to the gods in strength, the gods felt diffident to face him in a dual.

Then who is after all the cause of his ruin? She is the Mother Goddess Durgā or Kātyāyanī, who was born in the Vindhyan region and was propitiated by the pre-Aryan tribe. And her deification took place only much later. Because of Her pre-Aryan affiliation She expresses the Asuric motifs in unparalleled fashion. Through a bloody combat with Her Mahiṣāsura loses his stand. The Vedic gods reprsented by the Vedic Aryans seem to represent fascist mentality, but the Asuras seem to be socialistic in their outlook, for which they fall a prey in the hands of the Vedic people.

These redactors have gone to the extent of interpreting such struggle between the Asuras and the Devas as between the forces of darkness and light, a struggle, which is a permanent feature both in the micrososm and macrocosom as well. But they believe the victory of the gods as the win of civilization over savagery and triumph of the right over might.

The distinction between the Devas or the shining ones (Aryans) and the Asuras, the children of darkness is also well depicted in our religious symbolism. The Bhagavadgītā (Ch.16) tries to differentiate betwen the Devas and the Asuras in view of their inherent nature. The virtuous or ideal qualities in the society are accpted as godlike or Daivī and the opposite ones to be demoniac or Āsurī. Those diabolically fallen and damnably indifferent are believed to belong to Asura stock and the divinely good ones to Devas. Whatever may be the mystic interpretation, but the underlying fact behind it seems to be their utter difference in various walks of life.

Our faiths and beliefs, customs and traditions are medley of Aryan and pre-Aryan elements due to fusion of cultures. As a result we significantly mark the clear cut adoration of Mahiṣāsura with the Divine Mother Goddess during festive occasions. Ritual texts also right fully emphasise the position of Mahiṣāsura and enjoins mystic chants for his worship with the Mother Goddess. Our Artists and Sculptors, who are mostly gudied by Brahminical ideas, fashion the Asura variously. At times in theriomorphic form, or anthropomorphic one or the blending of both in one. Thus irrespective of age or region the icon of Mahiṣāsura changes.

The difference between the Devas and Asuras is cultural, social and religious which leads to their bitter attitude one towards the other. But in the social, cultural or religious sphere there is synthesis between these two people and even peaceful coexistence takes places in normal life due to marital relations and others, but these Brahminical redactors of the later period try to picture them differently.

BIBLIOGRAPHY

I. SANSKRIT TEXT (BY TITLE)

Abhilaśitārtha Cintāmaṇi. *Abhilaśitārtha Cintāmaṇi* of Somesvara Deva Part I, Ed. R.Shama Sastry, Mysore: University of Mysore Oriental Library Publications. Sanskrit Series No.69, 1926.

Agni Purāṇa. Ed. Baladeva Upādhyāya. Varanasi: Vidyavilasa Press, 1966.

Aitareya Brāhmaṇa. *Aitareya Brāhmaṇa* with the Commentary of Sāyaṇa. Ed. V.G. Apte, 2 Vols. Anandasrama Sanskrit Series No.32, Poona: Anandasrama Press 1930-1931.

Amarakosa. *Nāmaliṅgānuśāsana or Amarakoṣa* of Amarasimha with the Rāmāśrami (Vyākhyāsudhā) Commentary of Bhanuji Dikṣita (Rāmāsram), Ed. Haragovinda Sastri. The Kashi Sasnkrit Series 198. Varanasi: Chaukhamba Sanskrit Samsthan, 1982.

Arthaśāstra. *The Kauṭilīya Arthaśāstra*. Ed. & Trans. R.P.Kangle 3 parts. University of Bombay, Studies in Sanskrit, Psrakrti and Pali No.1, Bombay: University of Bombay, 1969 ff.

Atharvaveda. *Atharvaveda (Śaunaka)* with Padapātha and Sāyanācārya's commentary. Ed. Vishva Bandhu 5 vols. Hoshiarpur: Visheshvarananda Vedic Research Institute, 1960-1964.

Bṛhat ṭhākurapūjāpaddhati. Ed. Ārttatrāṇa Dāśa, Śyāmasundara Nayaka. Cuttack: Dharmagrantha Store.

Brahmavaivarta Purāṇa. Ed. V.G.Apte. 2 vols. Anandasrama Sanskrit Series No.102, Poona: Anandasrama Press, 1935.

Brahmāṇḍa Purāṇa. Ed. J.L. Shastri. Delhi: Motilal Banarsidass, 1973.

Bhagavadgītā. *The Bhagavadgītā.* Ed. and trans. S. Radhakrishnan. Bombay: Blackie & Sons, 1985.

Bhavisya Purāṇa. *Bhaviṣya Mahāpurāṇa*. Ed. Khemaraja SrīKṛṣṇa Dāsa. Bombay: SriVenkatesvara Press, 1959.

Bhāgavata Purāṇa. *Srīmadbhāgavata Mahāpurāṇam*. Gorakhpur: Gita Press, Samvat 2022.

Caṇḍiśataka. *Caṇḍīśatakam* of Mahakavi Bāṇabhaṭṭa. Rājasthāna Purātana Granthamala No.94, Jodhpur: Rajasthan Oriental Research Institute,1968.

Caturvarga Cintāmaṇi of Hemādri Vol.II, Part I Reprint, Ed. Bharata Canadra Siromani. Varanasi: Chaukhamba Sanskrit Samsthan, 1985.

Devībhāgavata. *Srīmad Devībhāgavatam*. Ed. Ramateja Pandey. Kāśī: Pandita Pustakālaya, 1969.

Devī Māhātmya. *Śrī Durgāsaptaśati.* Gorakhpur: Gita Press, Samvat 2027.

Devī Purāṇa. *Devī Purāṇam.* Ed. Pañcānana Tarkaratna. Calcutta: Parrot Press, Āṣāḍha 1384.

Durgā Pūjā. *Durgāpūjāṭattva* of Raghunandana Bhaṭṭāchārya. Ed. Satish Chandra Siddhantabhusana. Sanskrit Sahitya

Parishad Series No.5, Calcutta, Siddhesavara Press, Vaiśākha 1331 (1924).

Durgāpūjāviveka. *Durgāpūjāviveka* etc. of M.M. Śūlapāni and others. Ed. Satish Chandra Siddhantabhusana. Sanskrit Sahitya Parishad Series No.7. Calcutta: Siddhesvara Press, Āśvina 1331 (1924).

Harivaṁśa. *Mahābhārata-Khilabhāga-Harivaṁśa.* Ed. & Trans. in Hindi. Pandita Ramanārāyaṇa Datta Śāstrī Pandeya 'Rāma'. Gorakhpur: Gita Press, Samvat 2031.

Kālikā Purāṇa. *Kālikāpurāṇam.* Ed. Biśvanārāyana Śāstrī. Jayakrishnadas-Krishnadas Prācyavidyā Granthamālā No.5, Varanasi: Vidyavilasa Press, Vikram Samvat 2029 (1972).

Kālivilasa Tantra. *Tantrik Texts Vol.VI, Kālivilāsa Tantra.* Ed.Arthur Avalon & Parvati Caran Tarkatirtha. London: Luzac & Co. 46, Great Russell Street, 1917.

Kulacūḍāmaṇi Nigama. Ed. Arthur Avalon. Madras: Gaṇesh & Co., Private Ltd., 1956.

Kūrma Purāṇa. *The Kūrma Purāṇa* (with English translation). Ed. Anand Swarup Gupta. Tr. A. Bhattacharya, S. Mukherji, V.K.Varma, G.S. Rai. Varanasi: All India Kashiraj Trust, 1972.

Mahābhāgavata Purāṇa. *The Mahābhāgavata Purāṇa.* Text critically edited by Pushpendra Kumar. Delhi: Eastern Book Linkers, 1983.

Mahābhārata. *The Mahābhārata*. For the first time critically edited by Vishnu S. Sukthankar (and others) 19 vols. Poona: Bhandarkar Oriental Research Institute, 1933-1959.

Mahābhārata. Hindi Trans. Pt. R.N. Datta Shastri 6 volumes, 4th Edition Gorakhpur: Gita Press, Samvat 2030.

Maitrāyanī Saṁhitā. *Yajurvedīya Maitrāyaṇī Saṁhitā*. Ed. Sripāda Damodar Satavalakar. 4th edition. Paradi: Svadhyaya Mandala, 1983.

Mānasāra. *Mānasāra on Architecture and Sculpture*. Ed. P.K.Acharya. Allahabad: Oxford University Press, 1933.

Mārkandeya Purāna. *Mārkaṇḍeya Purāṇa*. Ed. Jibananda Vidyasagara. Calcutta: Sarasvati Press, 1879.

Matsya Purāṇa. Ed. Radheshyama Khemka. Gorakhpur: Gita Press, 1984 ff.

Nirukta. *The Nighantu and the Nirukta*. Ed. Lakshman Sarup. 2 vols. Delhi: Motilal Banarsidass, 1967.

Padma Purāṇa. *Padma Purāṇam*. Ed. M.C. Apte. 4 vols. Anandāśrama Sanskrit Series No.131. Poona: Anandāśrama Press, 1894.

Rāmāyaṇa. *The Vālmīki Rāmāyaṇa*. For the first time critically edited by G.H. Bhatt and others 7 volumes. Baroda: Oriental Institute, 1960-1975.

Rūpamaṇḍana. *Rūpamaṇḍana* of Srī Sūtradhara Maṇḍana. Ed. Balarama Srivastava. Varanasi: Motilal Banarsidass, 1964.

Ṛgveda. *Ṛgveda Saṁhitā with the commentary of Sāyaṇa*. Ed. N.S. Sontakke, C.G. Kasıkar. 5 Vols. Poona: Vaidika Saṁśodhana Maṇḍala, 1933-1951.

Śatapatha Brāhmaṇa. *The Śatapatha Brāhmaṇa, in the Mādhyandina Śākhā with extracts from the commentaries of Sāyaṇa, Harisvāṁin and Dvivedaganga.* Ed. Albrecht Weber. Varanasi: 1964.

Skanda Purāṇa. *Skanda Mahāpurāṇa.* Bombay: Venkatesvara Press, Saṁvat 2020.

Sāradātilaka. *Sāradātilaka Tantram.* Ed. Arthur Avalon. 2 parts. Calcutta: Āgamānusandhāna Samiti, 1933.

Śiva Purāṇa. *Śrī Śiva Mahāpurānam.* Ed. Ramateja Shastri Pandeya. Kasi: Pandita Pustakalaya, Samvat 2020.

Taittirīya Brāhmaṇa. *Kṛṣṇa Yajur Vediyam. Taittirīya Brāhmaṇam* 3 Volumes. Ed. N. Sastri Godbole. Anandāśrama Sanskrit Series No.37, Poona: Anandāśrama Press, 1979.

Varāha Purāṇa. *The Varāha Purāṇa* (with English translation). Ed. A.S.Gupta. Tr. Ahibhusan Bhattacharya. Varanasi: All India Kashiraj Trust, 1981.

Varaṣakriyākaumudī. *Varṣakriyākaumudī* of Govindānanda Kavikankaṇācārya. Ed. Kamala Kṛṣṇa Smṛtibhūṣaṇa. Calcutta: Asiatic Society of Bengal, 1901-1902.

Vāmana Purāṇa. *The Vāmana Purāṇa* (with English translation). A.S. Gupta, Tr. Varanasi: All India Kasiraj Trust, 1967.

Viṣṇudharmottara. *Viṣṇudharmottara Purāṇa.* Bombay: Venkateshvar Press, Samvat 1969.

Yajurveda. *Vājasaneyi-Mādhyandina-Śukla Yajurveda Saṁhitā.* Ed. Śrīpāda Dāmodara Satavalekar. Paradi: Svādhyāya Mandala.

II. SECONDARY WORKS (BY AUTHOR)

Agrawala, R.C. "A Terracota-Plaque of Mahishamadini from Nagar, Rajasthan". *Lalitakalā.* NSI-2 (April 1955-March 1986). 72-74., "Mahishamardini in Early Rajasthani Art", *The Researcher*, Vols. V-VI (1964-65): 11-15.

Agrawala, V.S. *A Catalogue of the Brahmanical Images in Mathura Art*. Lucknow: U.P. Historical Society, 1951, pp.57-58.

Banerjea, J.N. *The Development of Hindu Iconography.* Calcutta: University of Calcutta, 1956.

Banerjee, R.D. "The Temple of Śiva at Bhumara". *Memoirs of the Archaeological Survey of India.* No.,16, Calcutta: Superintendent, Government Printing India, 1924.

Banerji Sastri, A. "The Asuras in Indo-Iranian Literature" *JBORS*-XII, 1 (March 1926), pp.110-139.
"Asura Expansion in India" *JBORS*-XII 2 (June 1926), pp.243-285.
"Asura Expansion by Sea", *JBORS*-XII 3 (September 1926), pp.334-360. "Asura Institutions", *JBORS*-XII 4 (December 1926), pp.,503-539.

Bhandarkar, D.R. "Aryan Immigration into Eastern India". *Annals of the Bhandarkar Oriental Research Institute* XII (1931), 103-116.

Bhandarkar, R.G. *Vaiṣṇavism, Śaivism, and Minor Religious Systems.* Varanasi: Indological Book House, 1965 (Reprint of 1913 ed.).

Bhargava, P.L. "The Original Home of the Aryans and Indo-Iranian Migration". *Annals of the Bhandarkar Oriental Research Institute.* (1968),48-49, 219-226.

Bhattasali, Nalinikanta. *Iconography of Buddist and Brahminical Sculptures in the Dacca Museum.* Dacca: Dacca Museum Committee, 1929.

Brown, W.Norman. "Proselytizing the Asuras: A Note of Rgveda 10.12". *Journal of the American Oriental Society,* 39 Part 2 (1919): 100-103.

Chattopadhyaya .,Debiprasad. *Lokāyata-A Study in Ancient Indian Materialism.* 3rd edition, New Delhi: People's Publishing House, 1973.

Chattopadhya, K.P. *The Ancient Indian Culture Contacts and Migrations.* Calcutta: Firma K L Mukhopadhyaya, 1970.

Choudhary, Radha Krishna. *Vrātyas in Ancient India.* Varanasi:Chowkhamba Sanskrit Series Office, 1964.

Coburn, Thomas, B. *Devī-Māhātmya: The Crystallization of the Goddess Tradition.* With a Foreword by Daniel H.H. Ingalls. Delhi: Motilal Banarsidass, 1984.

Dandekar, R.N. "God in Hindu Thought" *Annals of the Bhandarkar Oriental Research Institute.* 48 & 49 (1968) 433-465. "Asura Varuna", *Annals of the Bhandarkar Oriental* Research Institure: 21 (1941): 1-35.

Dange, S.A. *Encyclopaedia of Puranic Beliefs and Practices.* 4 vols. Delhi: Navrang, 1986-1988.

Dasgupta, S.N. *A History of Indian Philosophy.* 5 vols. Cambridge University Press, 1922 ff.

Devasthali, G.V. *Religion and Mythology of the Brāhmanas.* The Bhau Vishnu Ashtekar Vedic Research Series, Vol.No.1, Poona: University of Poona, 1965.

Dhal, U.N. *The Glory that was Viraja Ksetra.* Delhi: Nag Publishers, 1984. "Mahisāsura Image in the Purāṇas". *Journal of the Oriental Institute* , M.S. University of Baroda, Vol. XXXVII, Nos.3-4 (March-June 1988),pp.215-219.

Divakaran, Odile. "Durgā the Great Goddess: Meaning and Forms in the Early Period". In Micheal W. Meister (Ed.) *Discourses on Śiva. Proceedings of a Symposium on the Nature of Religious Imagery.* Bombay: Vakils, Feffer & Simons Limited, 1984, 271-288.

Donaldson, T.E. *Hindu Temple Art of Orissa.* 3 vol, Leiden: E.J.Brill, 1987.

Elmore,W.T. *Dravidian Gods in Modern Hinduism.* First Reprint. Delhi: Asian Educational Services, 1984.

Fleet, J."Mahishamandala and Mahishmati". *Journal of the Royal Asiatic Society* (1910): 425-447.

Ghurye, G.S. *Gods and Men.* Bombay: Popular Prakashan Pvt.Ltd. 1962.

Gupte, R.S., Mahajan, B.D. *Ajanta, Ellora and Aurangabad Caves.* Bombay: D.B. Taraporevala Sons & Co. Pvt. Ltd., 1962.

Hale, Wash Edward. *Asura-in Early Vedic Religion.* Delhi: Motilal Banarsidass, 1986.

Jain Vasasisya K.L. *The Indian Asuras Colonised Europe.* Delhi: Itihasa Vidya Prakashan, 1990.

Karmarkar, A.P. *The Religions of India.* Vol.I, Lonavla: Mira Publishing House,1950

Kosambi, D.D. *Myth and Reality.* Bombay: Popular Prakashan Pvt. Ltd; 1962. *The Culture and Civilization of Ancient India in Historical Outline.* Fourth Impression. Delhi:

Vikas Publishing House Pvt. Ltd., 1976.

Kumar, Pushpendra. *Śakti Cult in Ancient India* (with special reference to the Puranic Literature). Varanasi: Bharatiya Publishing House, 1974.

Lalye, P.G. *Studies in Devī Bhāgavata*. Bombay: Popular Prakashan Pvt. Ltd., 1973.

Leuva, K.K. *The Asur - A Study of Primitive Iron-Smelters*. New Delhi: Bharatiya Adimjati Sevak Sangh, 1963.

Majumdar,R.C., Pusalker, A.D. etc. *The History and Culture of the Indian People*, 11 Volumes, Bombay: Bhartiya Vidya Bhavan, 1951-69.

Margabandhu, C. "A Stone Plaque of Mahisamardini from Amreli, Gujrat", (Off print supplied by the author).

Mircea Eliade. (Ed.) *The Encyclopedia of Religion*. 15 Volumes New York: Macmillan Publishing Company, 1987.

Misra, Vijayakant. *Mahishamardinī*. Delhi : Rajesh Publications, 1984.

Mitterwaliner, G.Von. "The Kuśāṇa Type of the Goddess Mahiṣāsuramardinī as compared to Gupta and Medieval Types". *The German Scholars in India*. Vol.II. Bombay. Nachiketa Publications Ltd., 1976, pp.196-213.

Nagar, Shanti Lal. *Mahishāsuramardinī in Indian Art*. New Delhi: Aditya Prakashan, 1988.

O'Flaherty, Wendy Doniger. *Śiva, The Erotic Ascetic* (1973 Reprint). New York: Oxford University Press, 1981.

Oppert, Gustav. *The Original Inhabitants of India*. First Indian

Reprint, Delhi: Oriental Publishers, 1971.

Panigrahi, K.C. *Archaeological Remains at Bhubaneswar*. Second Edition, Cuttack: Kitab Mahal, 1981.

Paranjpe, V.G. "Historicity of the Asuras mentioned in the Ṛgveda". *Annals of the Bhandarkar Oriental Research Institute*. Volume 56, Parts I-IV (1975): 195-200.

Rao, T.A. Gopinath. *Elements of Hindu Iconography*, Vol.I, Part II. Second Edition Delhi: Motilal Banarsidass, 1968.

Rocher, Ludo. *"A History of Indian Literature". The Purāṇas.* Vol.II, pt.3.-Wiesbaden: Otto Harrassowitz, 1986.

Sahai, Bhagwant. *Iconography of Minor Hindu and Buddhist Deities*. New Delhi: Abhinav Publications, 1975.

Seshadri, M. "Mahiṣāsuramardinī, Images, Iconography and Interpretation". In: Half-yearly *Journal of the Mysore University*, N.S. Section A-Arts. Vol.22. No.2 (1963): 1-28.

Shah, Priyabala. *Viṣṇudharmottara Purāṇa*. Third Khanda, Vol.II Baroda: Oriental Institute, 1961.

Shulman, David D. *Tamil Temple Myths: Sacrifice and Divine Marriage in the South Indian Śaiva Tradition*. Princeton: Princeton University Press, 1980.

Sircar, D.C. "Mahiṣamardinī Durgā". *Pof. P.B.Desai Felicitation Volume. Studies in Indian History and Culture*. Ed. S.Ritti, B.R.Gopal. Dharwar: Karnataka University, 1971, 155-162.

Soundara Rajan, K.V. "A Devi Cult Nucleus at Jagat, Rajasthan",

Vishvesharananda Indological Journal, Vol.I (1963), 130-140.

Srivastava, Balaram. *Iconography of Śakti. A Study Based on Śrī Tattvanidhi.* Chowkhamba Oriental Research Studies No.9, Varanasi: Chowkhamba Orientalia, 1978.

Tiwari, J.N. *Goddess Cults in Ancient India*. New Delhi: Sundeep Prakashan, 1985.

Venkatesvarn, C.S. "The Vedic Conception of 'Asura'." *The Poona Orientalist*. Vol.13 Nos.I and II (January 1948-October 1948): 57-60.

Whitehead, Henry. *The Village Gods of South India*. AES Reprint. New Delhi, 1983.

Yaduvamsi. *Śaivamata*. Patna: Bihar Rāṣṭrabhāṣā Parishad, 1955.

Zimmer, Heinrich. *The Art of Indian Asia*. Two Volumes. Ballingen Series 39. New York: Pantheon Books Icn. 1955.

INDEX

A

B

D

G

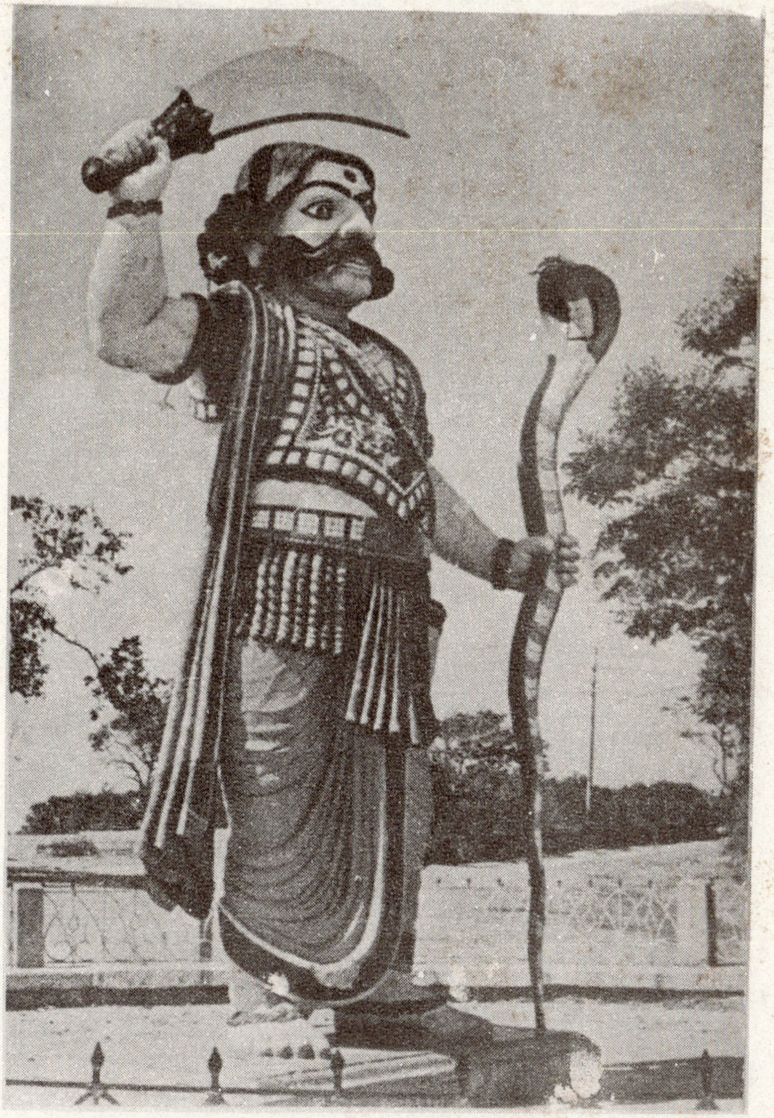

Fig.1

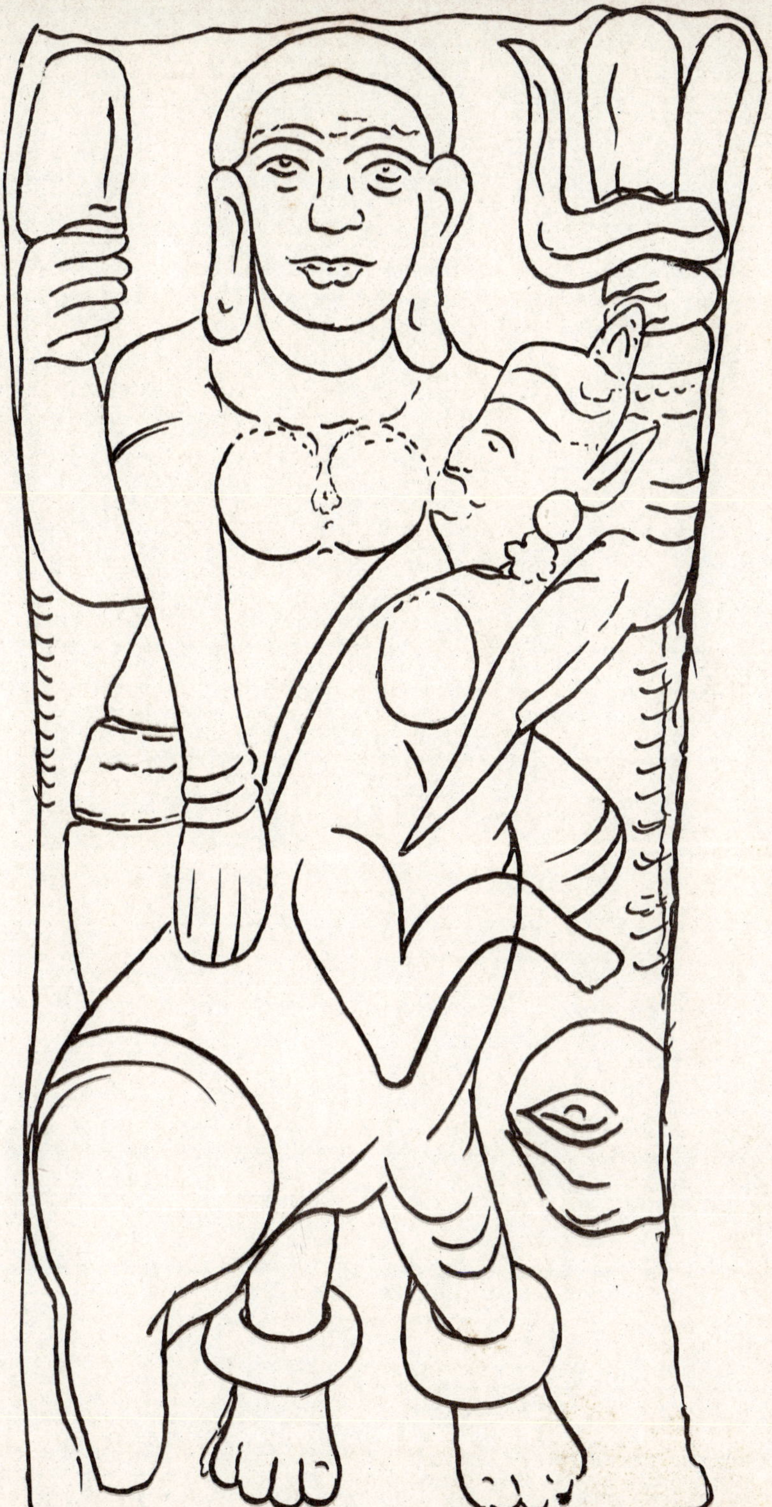

Fig.2

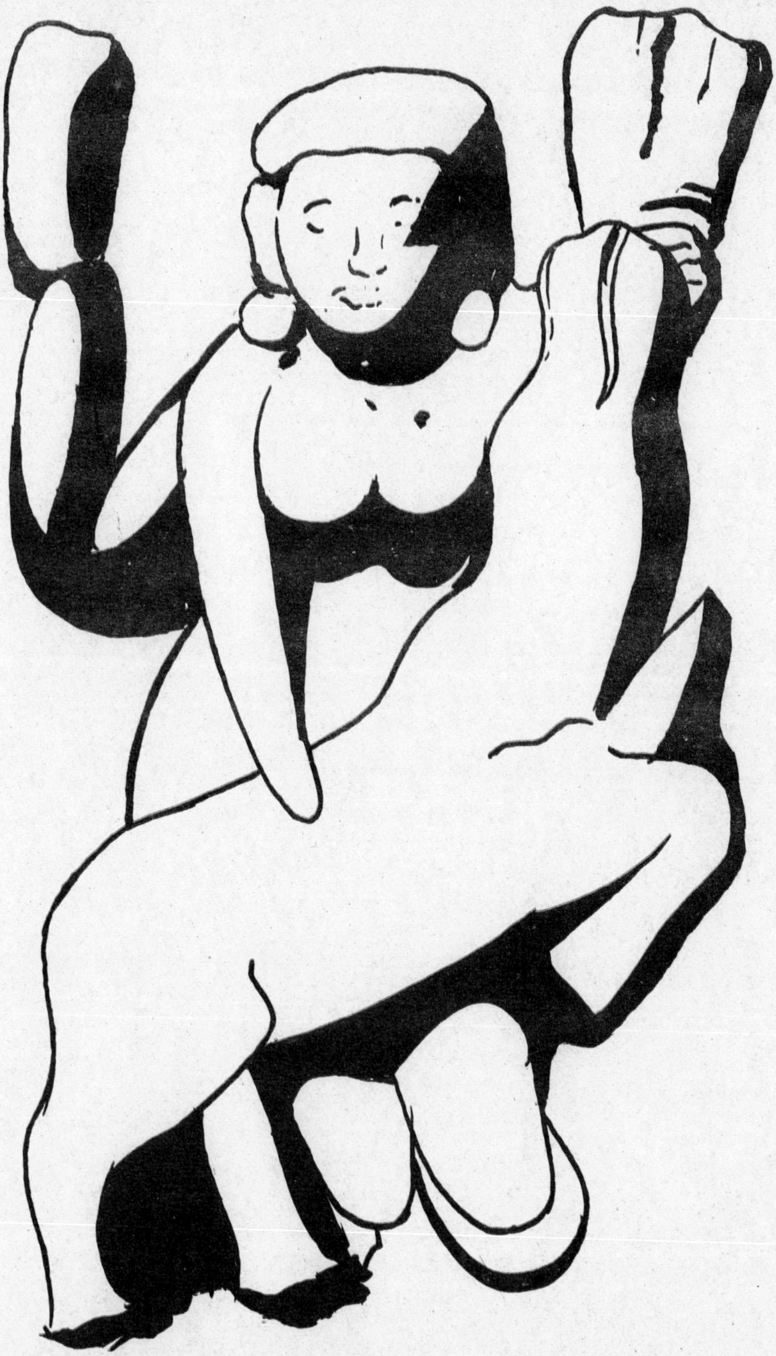

Fig.3a

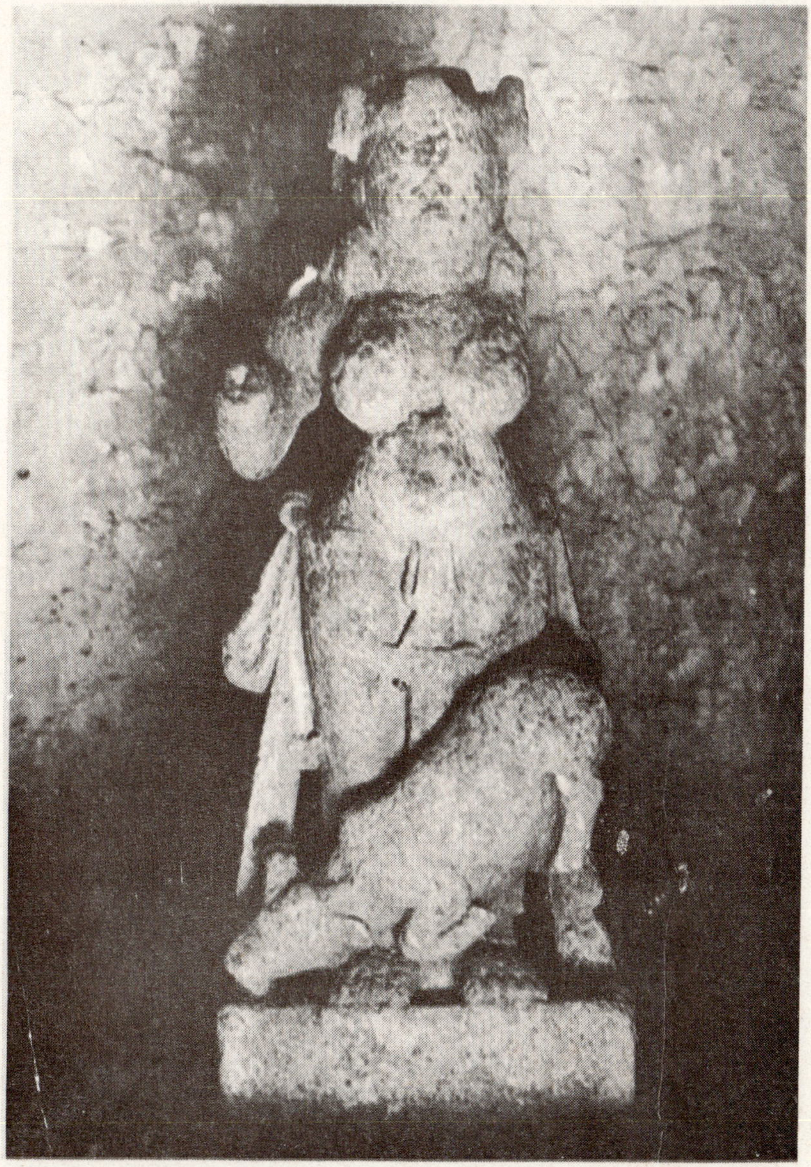

Fig.3b

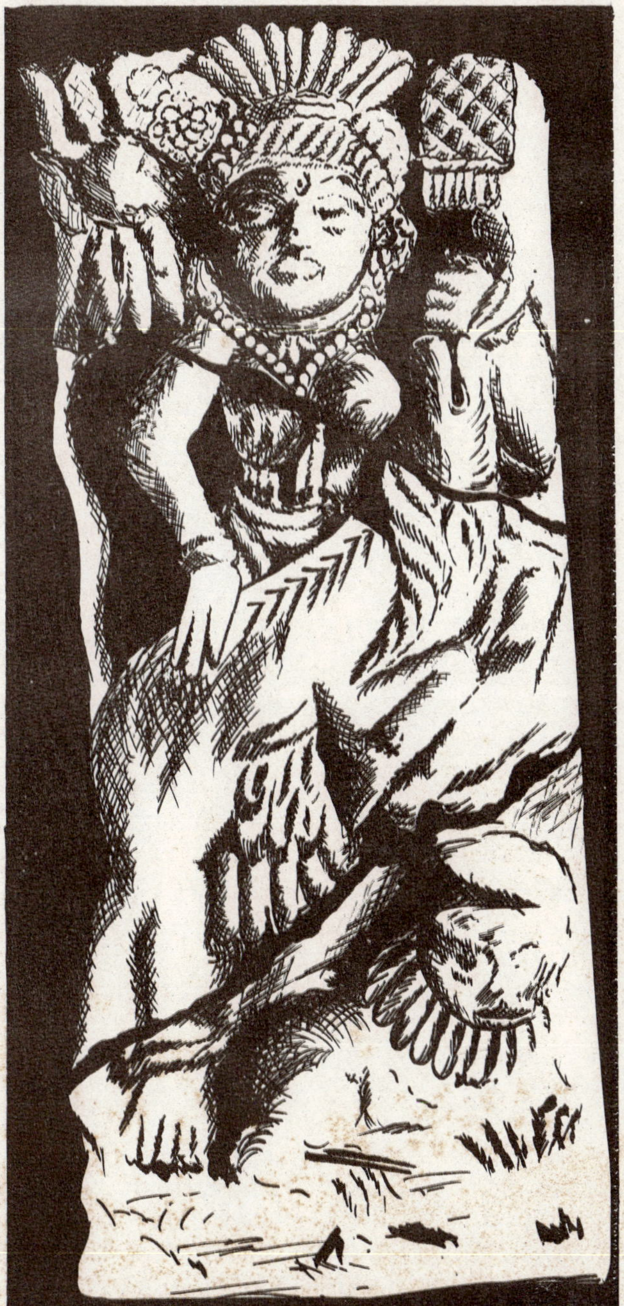

Fig.4a

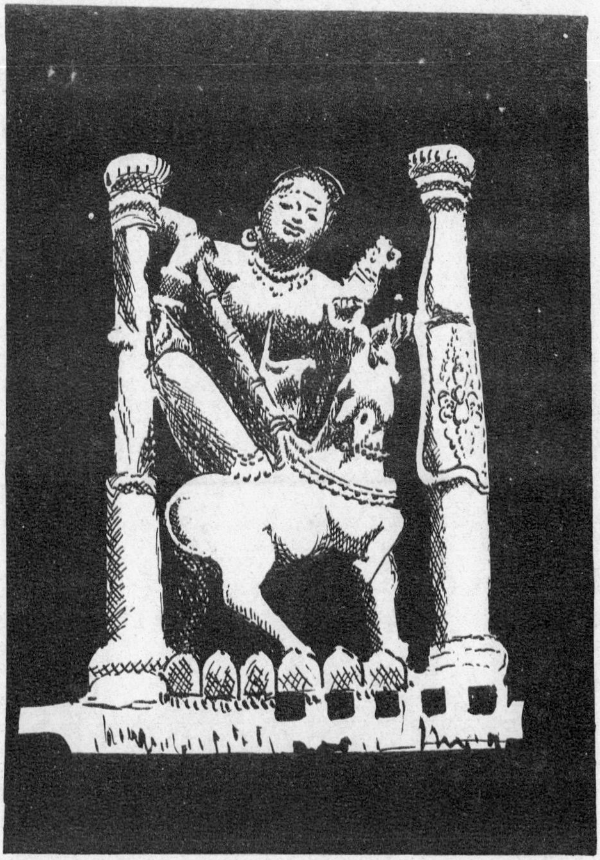

Fig.4b

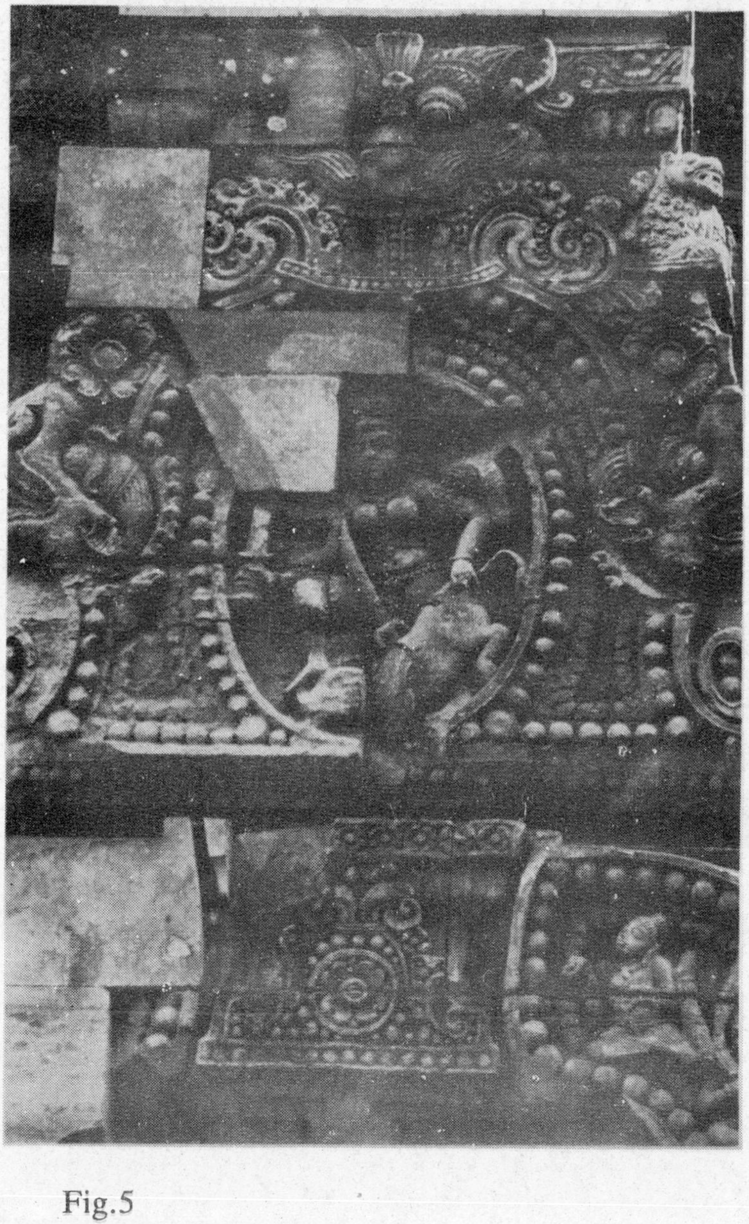

Fig.5

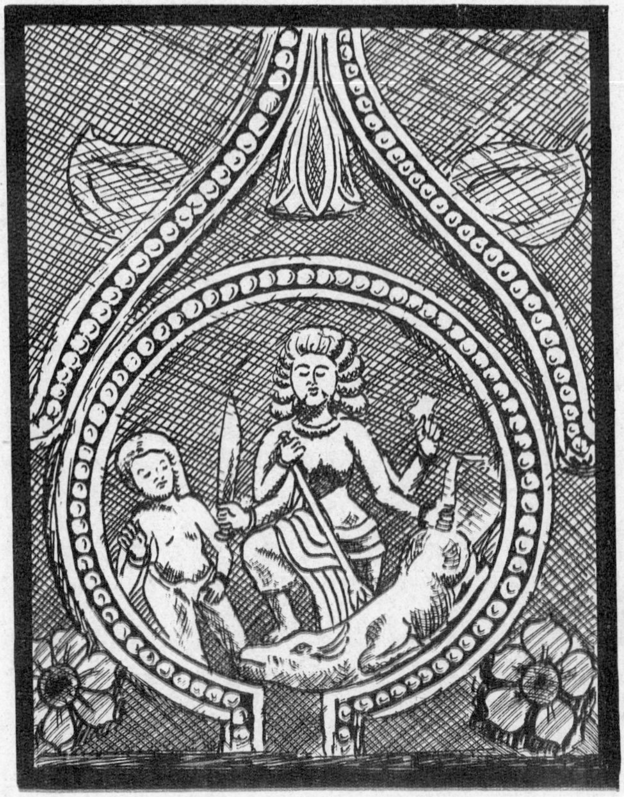

Fig.6

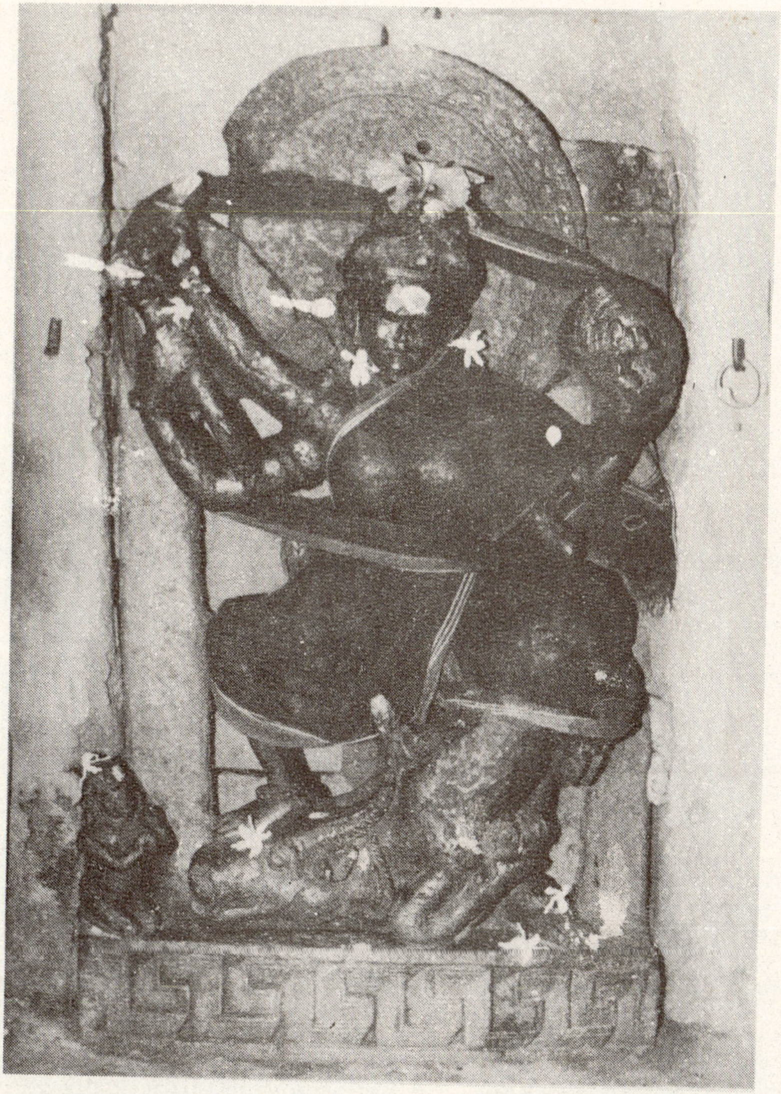

Fig.7

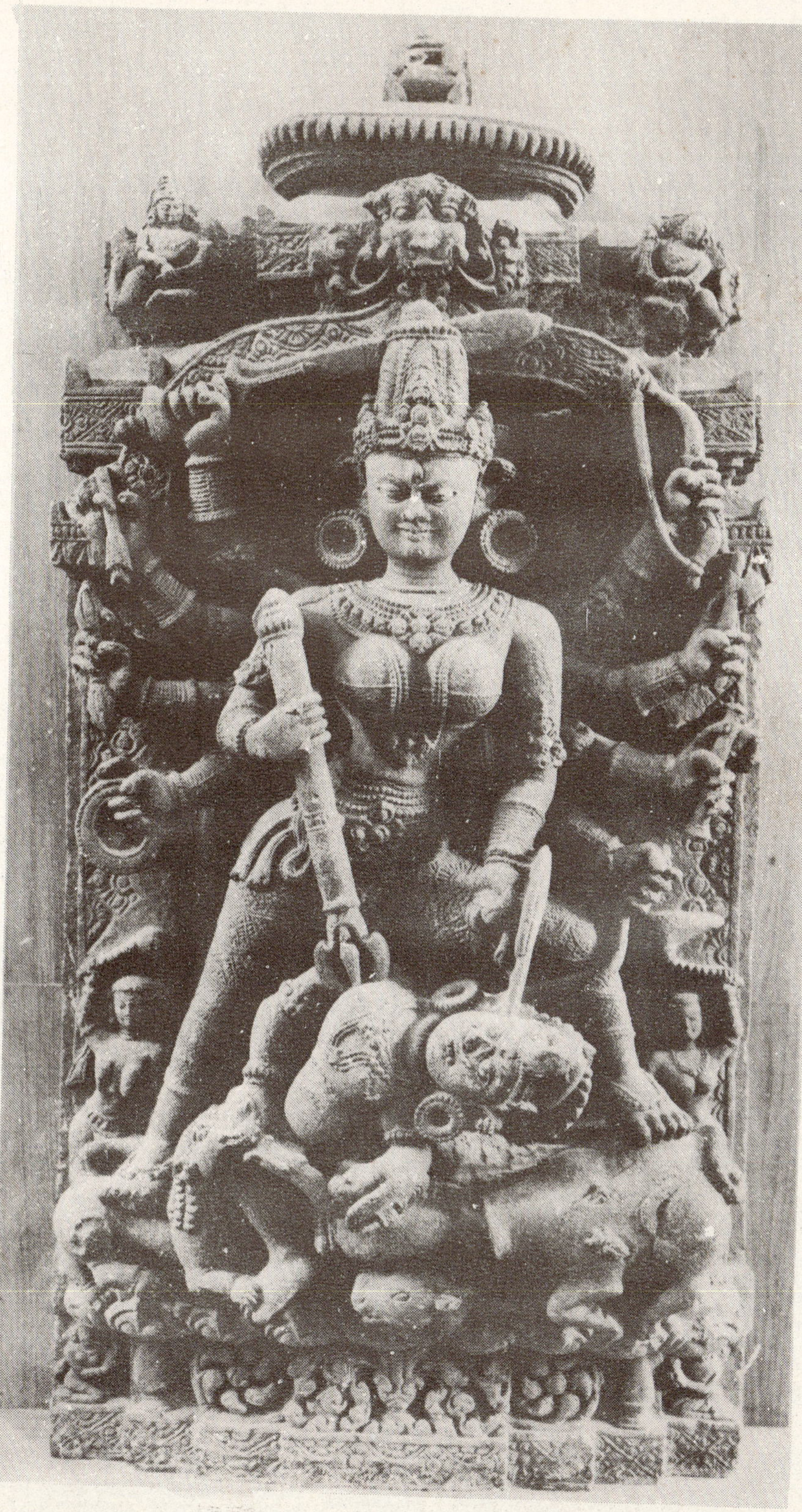

Fig.8a

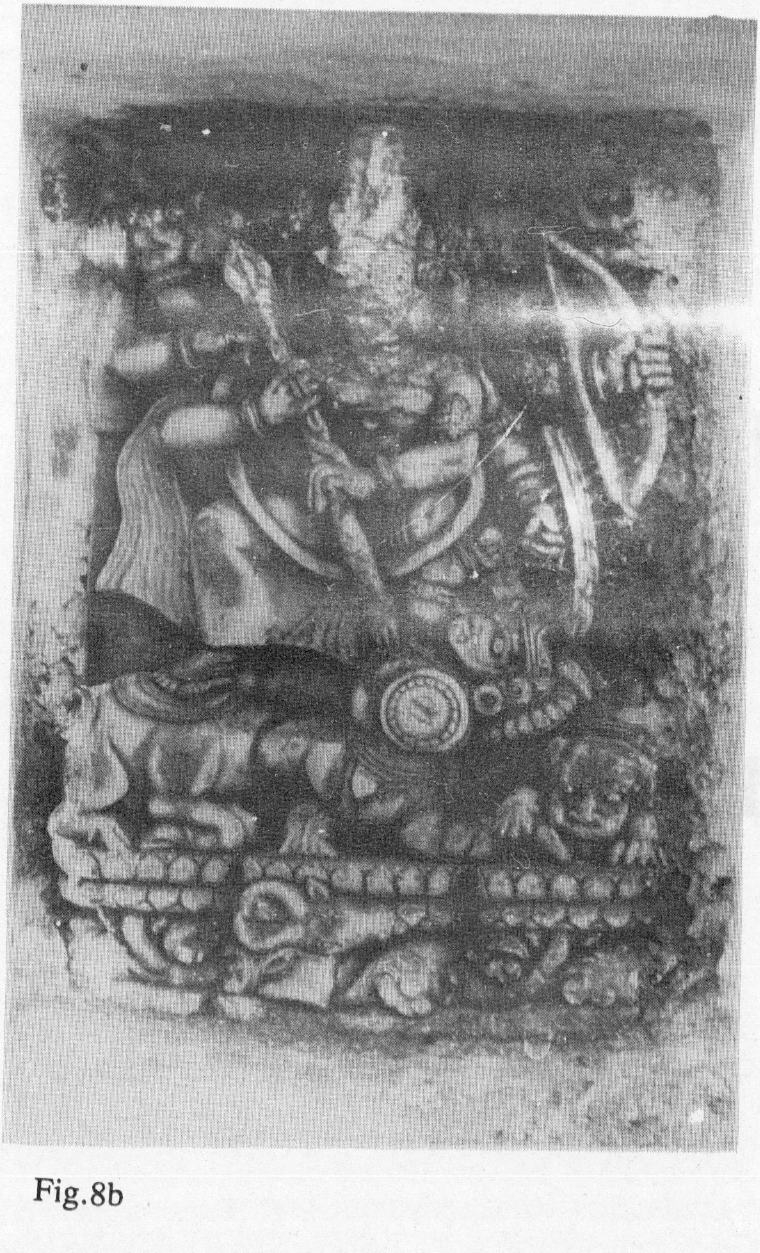

Fig.8b

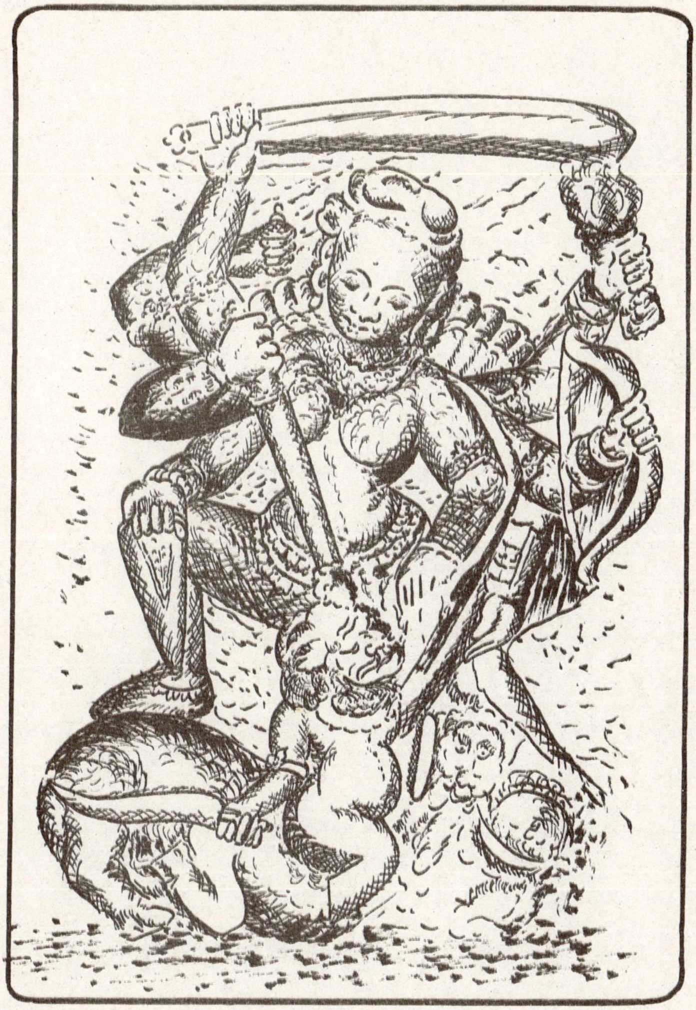

Fig.9

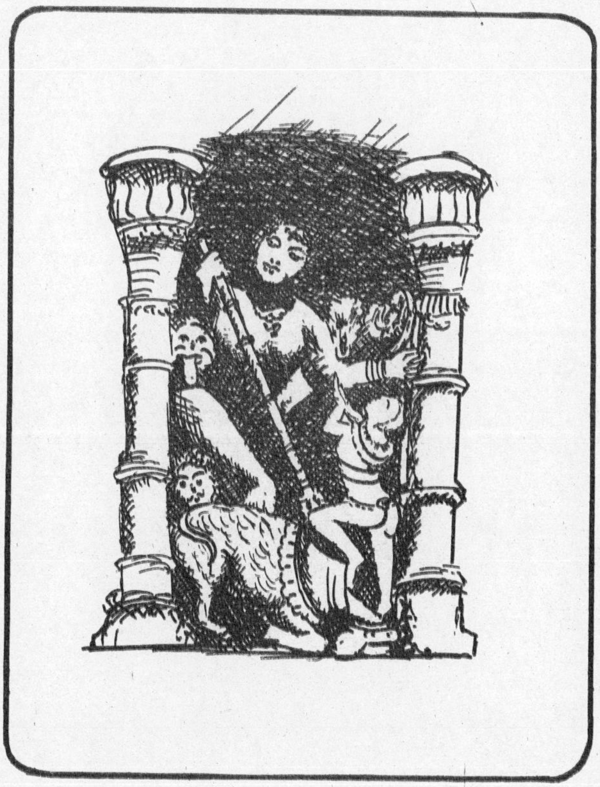

Fig.10

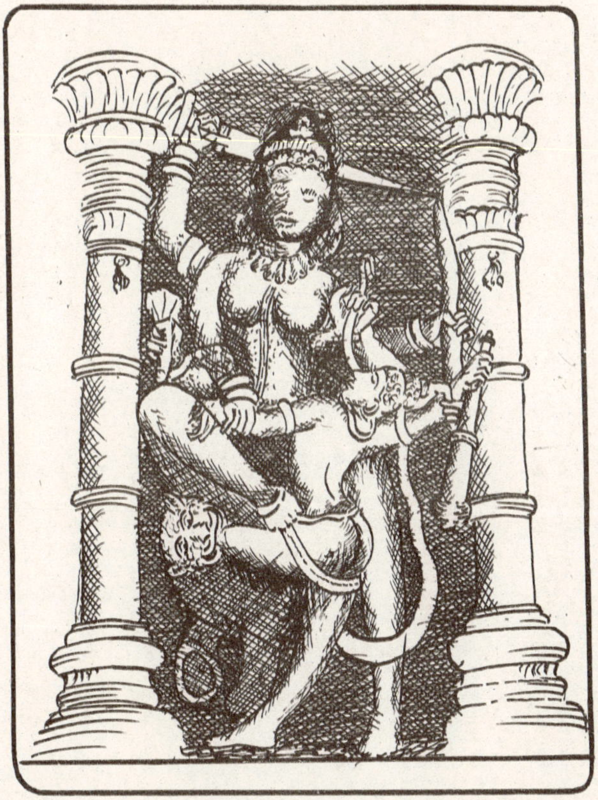

Fig.11

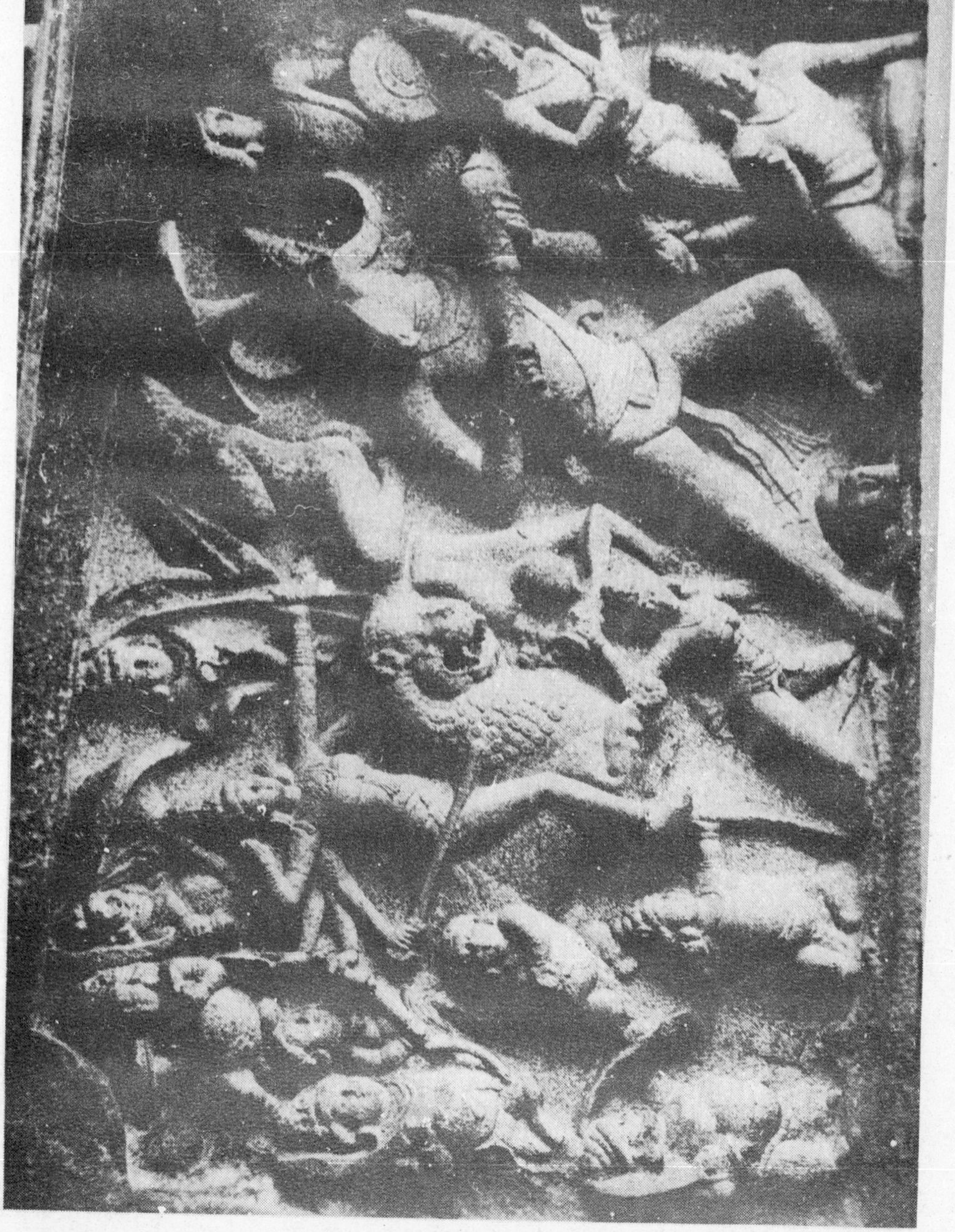

Fig.12a

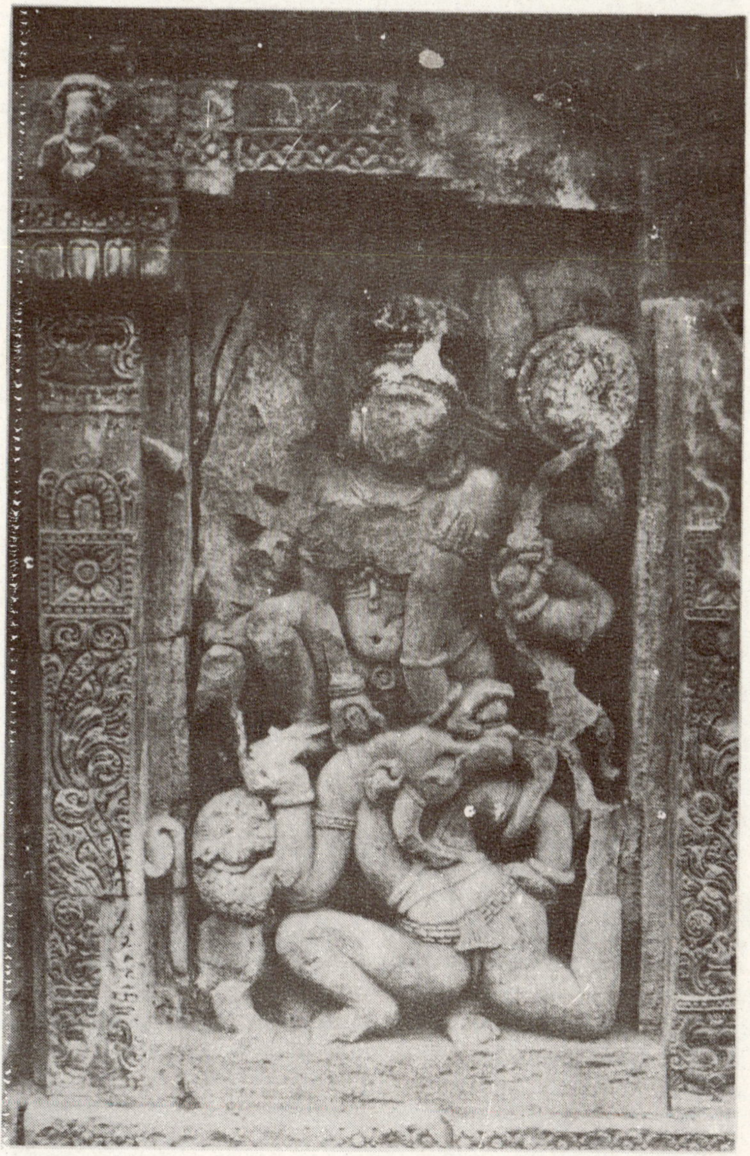

Fig.12b

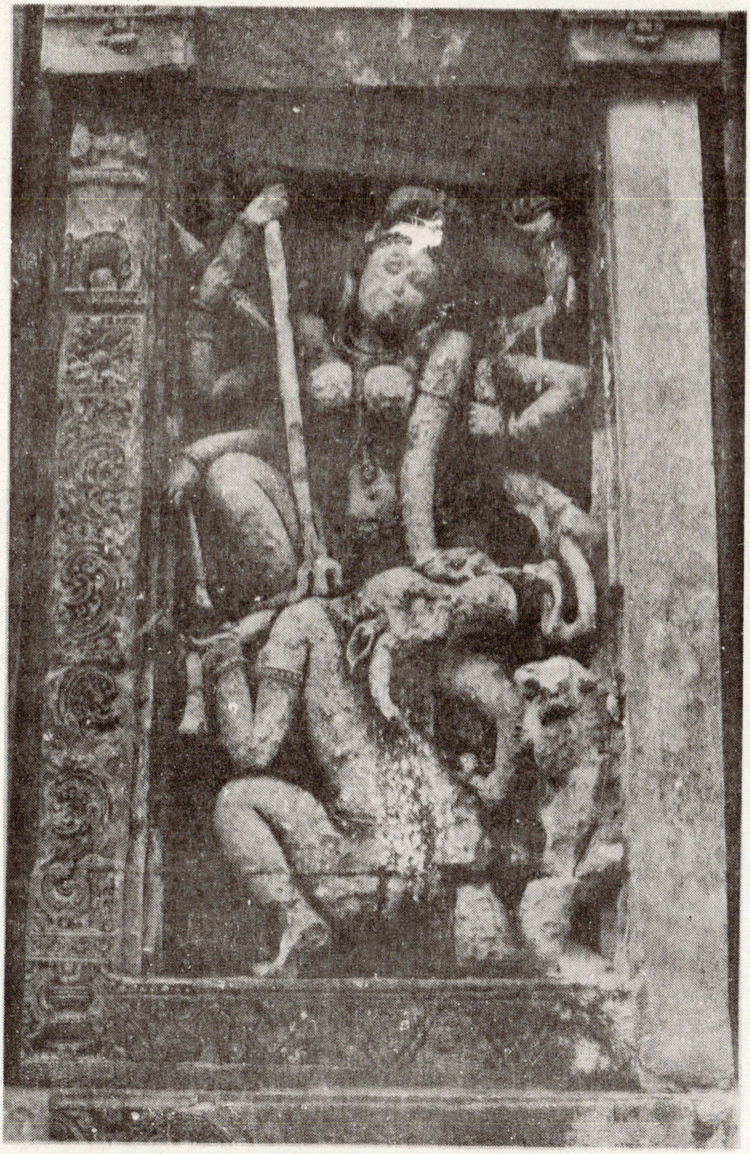

Fig.13

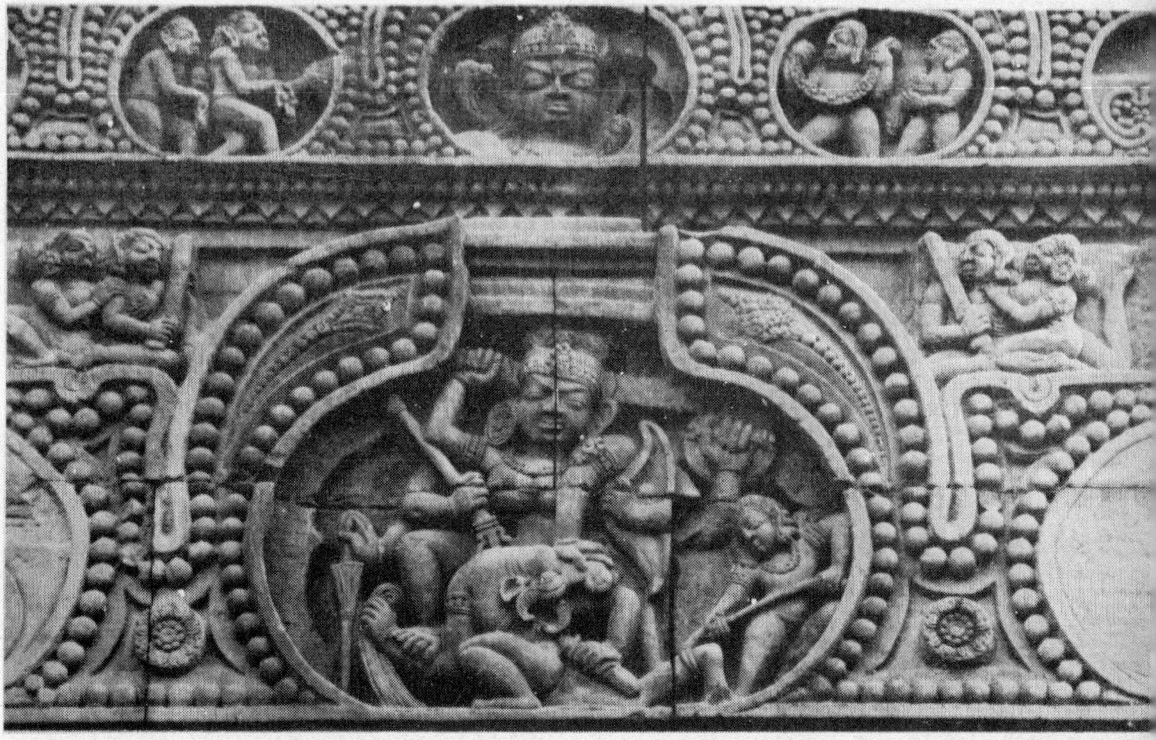

Fig.14a

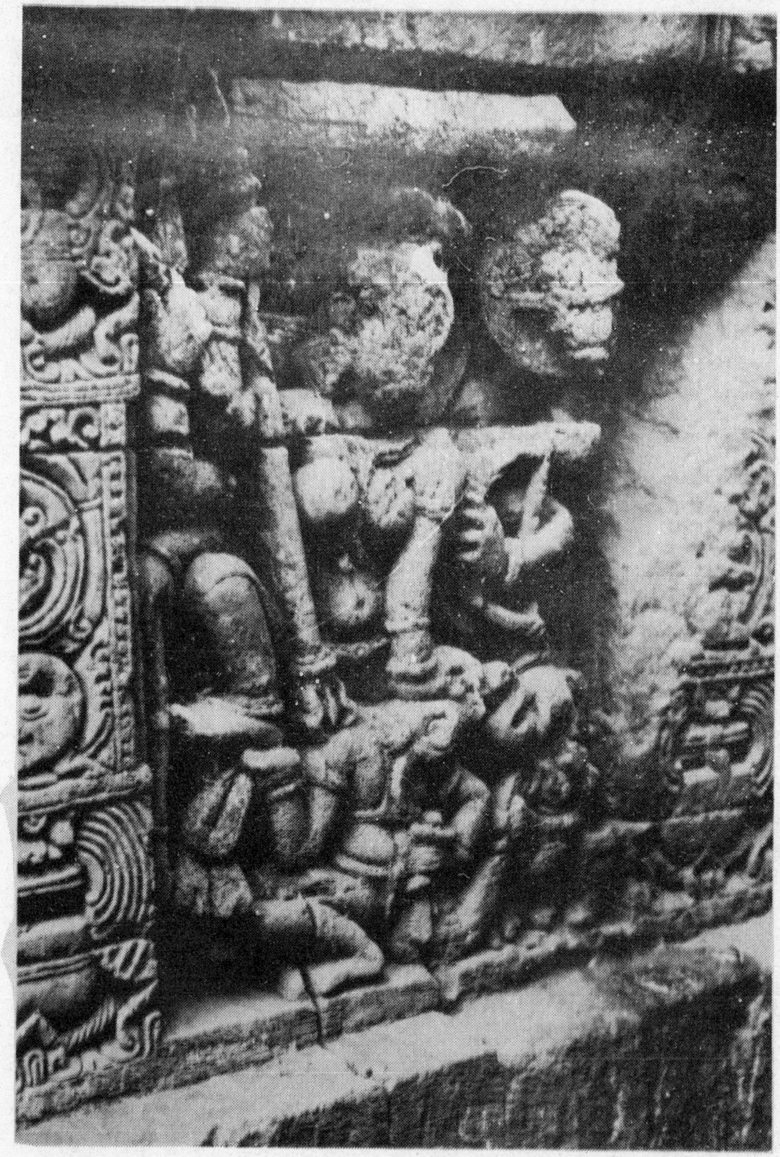

Fig.14b

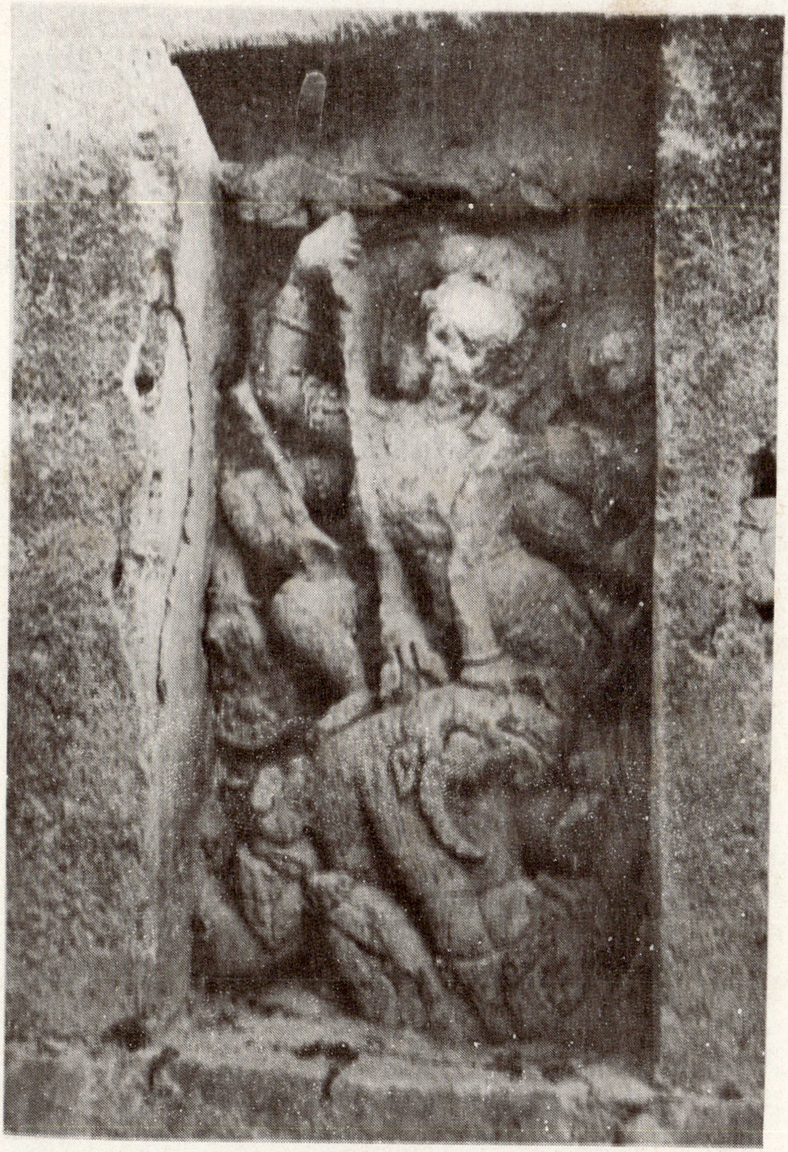

Fig.15